Leave a Well in the Valley

Turning Your Tragedies into Triumphs

Dale Peterson

www.xulonpress.com

To Teresa —

With God's Blessing!

Dale Peters
2010

Dedication

How can one begin to quantify the number of people who impact an individual in the course of a lifetime—from parents and grandparents, siblings, spouses, children, friends, extended family members, and even one's foes? It would seem that a book dedication should focus on one or more of those individuals who have influenced our growth and development in life or vocation the most.

Therefore, I want to dedicate *Leave a Well in the Valley* to my children, whom I love as much as life itself and of whom I am quietly but extremely proud: **Charity** Leigh, my first-born and near-perfect daughter; United States Marine Corps Captain **Justin** Dale Peterson, my career Marine, whose life was cut short by a freak accident in the sands of Al Anbar Province, Iraq; **Jordan** David, the brainiac of the five kids; United States Marine Corps Sergeant **Joshua** Daniel, who is like his father in so many ways it scares me; and **Joy** Rose, Daddy's girl.

To the five of you, I simply say that somewhere along the journey my focus changed—from wanting to be proud of you, to being so proud of each of you that words fail me, to hoping against hope that you could be proud of me as your dad. I love you!

Acknowledgements

In the process of writing, I have discovered that surely a book is not truly written by one individual alone, although one name may appear on the cover. Certainly this book cannot be credited simply to me, given the magnitude of the involvement and influence of others, especially those acknowledged below.

First, my wonderful wife Debbie, who has encouraged me to continue writing when giving up on this project would have been the greater relief at the moment, and for reading everything that I wrote, and doing so many times. Thanks for being so understanding during the evenings that you spent alone in the family room while I worked downstairs in my office.

Words cannot express adequately my gratitude to my younger brother Dennis, and editor for Bob Jones

University Press in Greenville, SC, who has worked relentlessly on the punctuation, grammar, and formatting of the manuscript from the beginning. Thanks for baby-sitting your older brother through a process that surely you must have thought would never end. I don't know how you work your editorial magic, but you do it well.

My younger sister Gina King must have driven the price of Kleenex stock higher as she read and advised me concerning the manuscript. Thank you, sweet sister, for your assistance and your tears.

My dear friend, former church member, and partner in ministry, David Brown, also lent his eye for details, catching mistakes, correcting context, and encouraging his former pastor. Thank you, not only for your assistance on the manuscript, but for the years of your friendship.

Then, to my best friend of forty years—Dave Brown—I cannot muster adequate words to thank you for being as close to me in my valleys as any human being could possibly be. Others who traverse the valleys of life should be as fortunate as I have been to have a stalwart friend such as you.

And finally, thanks to numerous friends who have encouraged me to translate my life experiences into a book that would potentially impact others who must also cross the valleys as they journey through life.

Foreword

THIS BOOK HAS BEEN DUG FOR YOU

Dale Peterson has written an incredibly provocative book that will *help* all believers who are going through trials or difficulties. He begins by reminding us that we all have unavoidable problems in life, we all will walk through valleys. Then he reminds us of an absolute necessity for people who go through valleys; they need water. Dale Peterson reminds us first we must dig a well to get water. Then second, we must leave our well for others who need water.

Jesus is the "water" that is necessary for life and survival. Without water we will die in the wilderness or valleys of life. Water nourishes and replenishes the life-giving energy we lose to the hot sun. Don't we all lose something when problems and trials sap our energy? Sometimes we need to replenish our resolve and strength at a well we have dug ourselves. Then sometimes we are renewed by a well dug by someone else who went before us on life's journey.

But there's another benefit of water. Water gives us satisfaction. Suppose we've worked hard in the sun, we are hot and tired and the heat has drained our energy. We may be tempted to give up or to quit. Whether we do or not, the thought is sometimes there. Then we take a cool drink of water. Ah . . . water is good! After a refreshing enjoyable drink of water we are ready to go again.

So when we dig a well and drink God's refreshing water, don't forget those who come behind you. Just as you met God and He solves your problems, just as you enjoy His water—His presence—don't forget about other people who need His presence. When you meet God, don't forget to leave a well so others can enjoy His presence.

Digging a well is important. It's hard, dirty, and sometimes it takes all the strength out of us. So our problems leave us exhausted and empty. Then we move beyond hard work to discouragement. But when we finally hit water—it's more than enjoyable. It's the greatest feeling in life. When God helps us solve our problems, it's the greatest experience at the time. But remember, others need what you have found—satisfaction. Leave a well of water for others. There can be no greater joy than helping others get the same satisfaction you have gotten from water – from Christ.

As a matter of fact, this book can make your life more enjoyable if you will leave a well for others that you originally dug.

I pray this book will change the way you look at difficulties. I pray you will find water and say, "Jesus . . . this water is good."

Elmer L. Towns
Co-Founder, Liberty University
Dean, School of Religion
Lynchburg, Virginia

LEAVE A WELL IN THE VALLEY

Table of Contents

INTRODUCTION

In a time when so many people are turning to the Internet, and when so few (comparatively) are reading actual books, I've asked myself, "Does the world really need another book?" However, after considering the number of people that I encounter each day—people who face the harsh realities of daily life with its myriad temptations, trials, and tribulations, I recognize that I really do have something to offer and from which many people can benefit. It's called *hope!*

The chapters and pages that follow are not merely autobiographical. Few people in this world know Dale Peterson or could care less who he is. However, everyone who lives must go through some valleys—and many of those valleys will be scary. Some of the valleys of life will rob us of emotional, mental, and physical energy.

At times, discouragement, despair, and even depression will threaten to overwhelm us.

This is a book about surviving the valleys—not merely surviving (although on some days even survival is a major victory!), but also gaining strength and victory as we emerge from one valley after another as travelers on the road of life. The valleys of life can offer valuable benefits if we deliberately choose to face forward, looking to our futures with faith and hope rather than backward in despair. And this isn't a "hope" that has no confidence. Quite the contrary. It is a hope that is well grounded in principles that have been proven by thousands—no, millions of travelers before you and me. But we can take advantage of these inexhaustible principles as we let go of our fears and embrace them with faith.

Sometimes, we are not willing to grasp that which can help us most because of our own fears. Much like the trapeze artist who swings from a platform high above the circus crowd, we cannot grasp the empty swing that will take us to the "other side" of the big top until we let go of the swing that we have in our hand. And, as the comedians say, "Timing is everything." We must judge quickly when to let go (of the past) to grasp the future. And for a few milliseconds, we have neither the "swing" of the past nor that of the future in our hands, as we choose to let go of the one to grasp the other.

Years ago, my friends Henry and Hazel Slaughter recorded a Gordon Jenson song reflecting a philosophy that has become a theme—a personal life goal—a determination for how I want to face the difficulties of life. I mean, if no one escapes pain in life—if each of us inevitably must enter the valleys of life—then isn't it wise to pre-determine how we plan to face the formidable inevitabilities of life? Shouldn't we set our hearts and minds to go beyond endurance and try to discover ways to *grow* through the experiences, not merely *go* through them?

The chorus of the Gordon Jenson song that the Slaughters brought home to my heart so vividly back in the early 1970's went like this:

Leave a well in the valley, the dark and lonesome valley;
Others have to cross this valley, too.
And what a blessing when they find the well of joy
you've left behind;
So, leave a well in the valley you go through.

That song finds its roots in the Old Testament—Psalm 84:6 says, "*Who* passing through the valley of Baca make it a well" (King James Version). Little seems to be written in depth about the valley of Baca, and even less appears to be understood about it. However, there are at least a couple of common (and key) elements concerning its meaning.

First, in Hebrew, *Baca* can be translated either "weeping" or "balsam trees." Or it could even be translated as "mastic shrubs." Both types of plants grow in dry or dessert places.

Second, the *valley of Baca* is also referred to as the "valley of tears," or the "valley of weeping," which seems to be referring to a place, perhaps a dry, sterile valley. Regardless of the specific translation, the prevailing idea is a grasp of a time and/or place of difficulty—that is, weeping or tears being associated with the meaning.

The culture of ancient Palestine usually dictated that, as shepherds nomadically moved their flocks from one pasture to another in search of adequate grass, they dig wells to ensure an adequate water supply for themselves and their flocks. However, it was customary when they moved on for them to fill in the wells they had dug.

Can you imagine the delight that a shepherd would experience when he not only discovered a green, fertile valley of grass for his flocks but also found an active well that someone else had labored to dig? What a relief it must have been to enjoy the reality of a well of refreshing water for a weary shepherd.

Perhaps you are going through a time of testing, trial, temptation, or torment—and are even wondering if you can survive. My friend, you can not only survive, but also thrive—if you will commit yourself, your survival, and your future to this simple goal:

I will use this present valley as a time of personal growth;
I will not waste the pain or the problem,
but will <u>grow</u> through it, not merely <u>go</u> through it.

The pages that follow offer the reader hope. Other people—this author included—have been through valleys similar to yours, and they have survived and succeeded. You can too. These pages contain insights and suggestions, practical steps that you can take that can prove helpful to you. You will be asked to accept a challenge as well—to determine that you will offer encouragement to others within the circle of your own influence as your heart hears and feels the pain of others around you.

The author uses the anecdotal approach to identify valleys in which he has personal experience—and personal victory in discovering the therapeutic value of the hope that comes from a fresh determination to face the future with faith—faith that God will not only lead you through your valley but also energize you as you "dig a well" in the valley through which you are passing.

This approach will be simple and refreshing. The author will identify common problems (or valleys) with which most of us may be faced in life. This is followed by an introduction of principles that can encourage and energize a weary traveler as he or she plods through the valleys of life. Finally, the author offers inspiration and hope.

Are you bogged down in a valley right now? Do you fear that a valley is on the horizon of your life? Are you struggling to come out of a valley? Take hope! Read on! You can make it!

1

When You Go Through A Valley

The problem/valley

"Dale, I have some terrible news for you concerning your parents and sister. On their way to church this evening, they were hit by a drunk driver—head-on. Gina is hospitalized, but is expected to recover. But, Dale, it doesn't look good for your mom and dad. You should come quickly!"

"I just wanted to let you know, I'm taking the kids and going to my mom's—I'm leaving you."

"Rev. Peterson, the prognosis is not good for your father—maybe he has six months to live."

"Reverend, my name is Dr. Lowell Roberts. I've just read your EKG and confirmed that you are having a heart attack."

***

That we will all go through "valleys" in life is a given. No one comes into this world and gets out again without going through some "valleys." Everyone goes through them sooner or later. Sometimes we create our own valleys by our decisions, whether we intend to do so or not. For example, some health issues may overtake us because in the day-to-day of life, we may have become careless. Sooner or later, a lack of exercise and a proper diet can bring about serious health problems, from diabetes to heart disease. On the other hand, some of us are genetically predisposed to certain physical maladies, such as heart disease or certain types of cancer.

At other times, and without warning, life can catapult us into a valley. It may be that a husband and father, faithful in the execution of his vocational responsibilities, finds that employer cutbacks and layoffs unexpectedly cost him his job through no fault of his own. It might be that a fatal car accident unexpectedly snatches a son or daughter from us. Or it could be that a faulty furnace causes a fire that reduces the family home to ashes. Perhaps a cherished relationship is dashed to pieces by a friend or spouse and feelings of betrayal and loneliness overwhelm.

Then again, there are other times when we see the problems developing, growing in size and intensity as they come at us. Perhaps it is one of our children. A parent may have a teenager who is exhibiting negative behaviors that would worry any parent. The parent watches almost daily changes as the teen becomes increasingly rebellious and uncooperative at home. As a student, his or her grades begin to suffer. Concerned teachers send notes home. It seems that childhood friends are being replaced with new friends. The son or daughter is listless, unmotivated, and argumentative. Perhaps money is missing in the family home. Increasingly the discussion of the now-worried parents turns to concern that illegal drugs may be involved—and then the phone call comes from the police station. The teenage son or daughter has been arrested.

Sometimes problems blind-side us unexpectedly in other ways. We take a young child to the doctor for something we think is rather routine, perhaps a visit for some antibiotics to help get rid of "a cold." However, the physician wants to do some blood work "just to be safe." But that blood work leads to additional testing, then to a specialist and more elaborate testing. Within thirty days of a "routine visit" to the family doctor, and after thousands of dollars of tests, the devastating news comes that the child has a very serious, even incurable disease.

For almost four decades now, I have walked in such valleys with others as I've stood beside caskets and grave sites—whether it's a young couple burying their beautiful baby daughter who died during the birthing process, or grown children as they bury their mother or a husband or wife as he or she sits in disbelief for the funeral service of a spouse.

The valleys are out there and there no doubt will be other valleys just over the horizon for you and me as pilgrims, passing through this world to the next. We must confront that reality, that inevitability.

This author believes that we must plan ahead, even for the surprises that will certainly overtake us in the course of our lifetime. If we selfishly concern ourselves only with what happens *to* us, we will unfortunately learn some lessons at great cost. The question is not *what* is going to happen *to* me that will cause a "valley experience" in my life but what do I want to happen *in* me *when* I go through the valleys? I may not always get to "choose" the valleys in life, but I can choose my own attitude and what happens *in* me.

The solution

With those thoughts as a backdrop, let's return to the idea of leaving "a well" in the valley. Before we get *to* the "valley," whatever valleys life might hand us, we must determine how we plan to act, react, respond, and grow through the experiences. We may not always succeed exactly the way we plan to, for the righteous man may fall down seven times, but we must determine in advance that we will rise up again (Proverbs 24:16).

A few years ago, my whole world turned upside down because of a divorce. In a short time my life appeared to be in total disarray. My job was gone—I resigned my pastorate, rather than put a great church through the trauma that would surely influence them. Many of my personal friends were in that church—and I was walking away as their pastor, only to discover that many of my closest friends didn't know what to say or do—and of necessity I was "leaving them" but didn't want them to leave me. Ethically, I didn't think it was advisable to pursue their friendships, since they would soon have another pastor—someone who would not appreciate the former pastor's cultivating the relationships with "his" people. Because I lived in a parsonage owned by the church, I had to vacate the house where our family had lived throughout the 1990s.

Like a weary boxer, I had been knocked down and was on the mat. In the distance, I could almost hear the referee counting: "Four, Five!" I felt like staying down—on the mat—most days. "Six, Seven. " But something inside me knew that the *right* thing to do would be to get up, chart a fresh new course, and proceed with life.

At a national conference in the Washington, D.C., area, shortly after my divorce, Dr. Vic Jungkurth, a pastor acquaintance then living in Columbus, Ohio—a man who has since become a source of great encouragement and strength to me—said, "Dale, you've had a train wreck, and it has put you in a proverbial wheelchair. Do you think you'll ever try to get up and walk again?" (He was playing the devil's advocate with me.

He was trying to get me to think strategically about the future—to resolve within myself to get up and go again.)

Since there isn't a big demand for divorced Baptist preachers, to arise and continue within my vocational field—whether as a pastor of a local church or in some other ministerial capacity—would be swimming upstream. I knew that fact well from many conversations with clergymen through the years. So in my own thinking, I came back to the song that my friends Henry and Hazel Slaughter sang years ago—"Leave a Well in the Valley." That song offers a great focal point for not only *surviving* the valleys of life but also *succeeding* as we come through them.

So first and foremost, we must determine that we will survive. We can exercise hope—a hope that is rooted in scripture, in the promises of God to His children, rather than in mere human strength alone. However, this demands that we determine within ourselves that we will do more than just survive, but that we will bless others in some way—that we will "leave a well in the valley" we go through. This requires an understanding on our part that we aren't the only travelers through the valley; "others have to cross this valley, too!"

The Stamina: Practical application of the solutions

Light begins to appear at the end of our tunnels in life as we determine within our own hearts and minds that we will survive, that we can go on, that there is a solution to our difficulty, dilemma, or depression. But it really isn't enough to merely *survive*—we must get in touch with determination to *thrive* on the other end of our valley. Taking this long view is a vital element to the strive-to-survive-and-thrive process.

This isn't thoughts tied to emotion. Quite the contrary. These are thoughts that transcend emotion that so easily overwhelms one during an experience in the valley. Valley emotions tend to dwell on the negative—feelings of defeat, discouragement, and even despair. All of those feelings drag us down and sit on our chests until we feel like we can't even breathe!

Emotional and spiritual stamina begins with the tiniest seed-thoughts of hope deep within the recesses of our hearts and minds. Stamina germinates as we feebly reach up in our mind's eye and grasp that seemingly remote possibility that we *might* survive if God will help us.

Some people tend to live by the concept that "God helps them who help themselves," and I think I comprehend what they're trying to say. But somehow, that philosophy is man-centered. However, adopting a God-centered perspective allows one to trust God (for the things beyond our control or ability) while recognizing and assuming personal responsibility. It can be viewed as a two-fold responsibility—God's part and man's part. Man *cannot* do God's part; and God *will not* do man's part.

As we plod through the valley experiences of life (step one) (and plodding sometimes takes every ounce of energy we have), we must lift our heads and eyes, looking ahead to the future (step two), determining to survive (step three). And when we have survived, we will find a way to use our experience to help others (step four). In other words, we deliberately choose, in advance, to "leave a well in the valley!"

What pain plagues you at this time in your journey along the road of life? What storm has blown into the once-quiet harbor of your heart? What valley has brought you low and nearly drowned you in despair?

STOP! Set it all aside for a moment. Read aloud the following:

Leave a well in the valley, the dark and lonesome valley;
Others have to cross this valley, too:
And what a blessing when they find the well of joy
you've left behind,
So, leave a well in the valley you go through.

You may feel as though you're drowning in a sea of sorrows. But in the privacy of your own heart, mind, and soul will you reach out and grasp that little chorus as though it was a life preserver, tossed to you from the hand and heart of another traveler who understands—experientially—the feelings of your failures, the despair of your doubts, and the panic of your predicaments?

You *can* survive, my friend! And when you have done so, you're then positioned to thrive.

Scriptures on Which to Meditate

(John 15:4-10, New Living Translation)

Remain in me, and I will remain in you. For a branch cannot produce fruit if it is severed from the vine, and you cannot be fruitful apart from me. "Yes, I am the vine; you are the branches. Those who remain in me, and I in them, will produce much fruit. For apart from me you can do nothing. Anyone who parts from me is thrown away like a useless branch and withers. Such branches are gathered into a pile to be burned. But if you stay joined to me and my words remain in you, you may ask any request you like, and it will be granted! My true disciples produce much fruit. This brings great glory to my Father. "I have loved you even as the Father has loved me. Remain in my love. When you obey me, you remain in my love, just as I obey my Father and remain in his love. I have told you this so that you will be filled with my joy. Yes, your joy will overflow!

(Psalm 86:1-7 New Living Translation)

Bend down, O LORD, and hear my prayer; answer me, for I need your help. Protect me, for I am devoted to you. Save me, for I serve you and trust you. You are my God. Be merciful, O Lord, for I am calling on you constantly. Give me happiness, O Lord, for my life depends on you. O Lord, you are so good, so ready to forgive, so full of unfailing love for all who ask your aid. Listen closely to my prayer, O LORD; hear my urgent cry. I will call to you whenever trouble strikes, and you will answer me.

(Psalm 23:4, New Living Translation)

Even if I walk through a very dark valley, I will not be afraid, because you are with me.

2

When Parents Die

The Valley

The evening service of the Broadway Baptist Church was under way. The congregation had opened the service that particular Sunday evening with enthusiastic, joyful singing. The ushers were receiving the evening offering when John Paul Johns, one of the deacons, came to the platform and said, "Preacher, you have an emergency telephone call from Knoxville on the phone in the lobby." I turned to the late-L.G. Williams and asked him to lead the congregation in singing until I could return to the platform.

The woman on the other end of the phone identified herself as Joan Peace, the wife of the pastor of the Temple Baptist Church of Powell, Tennessee. She informed me that my mother, father, and younger sister had been involved in a serious car accident while they were driving to church that evening for choir practice. Mrs. Peace somberly said, "Dale, they [the emergency room doctors at St. Mary's Hospital in Knoxville] don't expect your mother to make it, and your dad is also in serious condition. You need to come quickly."

My sister Gina, who had been driving, was also in the hospital, but according to Mrs. Peace, the hospital staff said she was in stable condition. I asked if anyone had been able to inform my brother Dennis, a school teacher at that time in southeastern Pennsylvania. Mrs. Peace replied that no one knew how to reach him on such short notice.

After assuring her that I would take that responsibility and thanking her for her call, concern, and prayers, I returned to the service in my own church in Paducah, Kentucky. The congregation was just concluding a song as I returned to the platform, so I was able to go immediately to the podium and convey to the congregation the contents of my conversation with Mrs. Jerry Peace. Their reaction was sober and somber.

Thankfully, that evening my best friend of at least a decade at that time—Dr. David Brown—was preaching for me, so I introduced him, let the congregation know that after the song I was scheduled to sing next, I was going to excuse myself from the service and try to reach my brother in Sellersville, Pennsylvania. Following that announcement, I picked up a hand-held microphone and sang the planned song—"I Don't Know About Tomorrow!"

That song communicates a critical principle on which we should focus, especially as we traverse any valley of life. But we'll come back to that later in the chapter. After singing, I excused myself, and my dear friend Dave Brown led the congregation in prayer for my family, particularly my parents and sister, and delivered the message that God had laid upon his heart that evening.

At the close of the service, someone took my eight-year-old daughter Charity and six-year-old son Justin somewhere in Paducah to eat dinner, while my wife Gina and I ran home to prepare for a hasty emergency trip to my home town of Knoxville, some six hours from Paducah. Late Sunday evening, our family headed toward St. Mary's Hospital in Knoxville. The children slept while I drove.

Arriving at the Intensive Care Unit (ICU) of St. Mary's Hospital in the wee hours that Monday morning, and knowing that my mother (Hazel) was in greater danger than my father (Ralph), I went straight to the nurses' station, identified myself, and asked to see my mother.

I'll never forget the scene in that ICU. The person in the bed did not even resemble my petite mother who had seldom ever weighed more than 98 pounds and was no doubt under that body weight at the time of the accident since she had been battling breast cancer for several months. Her body was swollen beyond recognition. Her head appeared as though it were a basketball with a face painted on it. Wires and tubes of numerous life-support systems were running everywhere. Had I not been in other ICUs numerous other times in my life as a pastor visiting other families, I think I might have "freaked out."

At about 11:00 a.m. that Monday morning, my brother Dennis and his wife Connie arrived. The scene was almost more that they could bear. I'm not sure how many times my brother could even go back into ICU and bear to see our mother in that condition.

[Dale, his sister Gina King, and brother Dennis]

That morning, as each of the doctors came through ICU on their rounds, I spoke with them and enlisted their cooperation in keeping me informed of every detail. They even gave written orders for the nurses to keep me informed of even the slightest changes—something that was almost never done that way. But the doctors understood my role as a veteran pastor and believed that I could make communication easier on them and more effective for our extended family.

As the medical community kept me informed, I kept our dad informed of every detail. Letting him know the results of the brain scans, which each time came back "no activity," was especially difficult. I'll never forget the conversation that I had with him following the second of the typically three brain scans.

"Dad, they're running a second brain scan today. If there is no brain activity today, they will typically run one more. If there is still no activity, they will be looking to us as a family to make a decision concerning life support."

Dad was never one to respond quickly with words, so before he could speak, I continued. "And Dad, this kind of decision isn't mine to make, even as the oldest son. This isn't even a decision that we as the children should make, but rather a decision that is *yours* to make, Dad—but we want you to know that we're going to back you, no matter what decision you make."

I can still see Dad's lower lip quivering as he looked me in the eye and calmly said, "Son, that decision has already been made. Your mother and I talked about this last Friday when we got home from her chemotherapy treatment [for the breast cancer, which had spread]. She didn't want to live like that."

On Thursday, following the automobile accident on Sunday, the medical staff ran that third brain scan. It showed no brain activity. In fact, the last response from Mom that I personally observed was when my younger brother Dennis arrived from Pennsylvania. When he and I walked into the ICU, I told Mom that Dennis and Connie had made it into town and that he was there with me in the room. I remember her struggle to somehow respond, but we reassured her that she didn't need to respond—just relax and rest.

Late in the day Thursday, it was agreed that if no positive changes occurred in mother's condition, all life support would be removed Friday morning. I was there, holding Mother's hand, as various devices and medical appliances were removed. In a matter of minutes, respiration slowed, heart rate slowed, the monitor alarm went off as Mom's heart "flat-lined," and the doctors pronounced her dead.

Why do I share that story with you?

For most of us, it is inevitable that we will bury our parents sooner or later, but it's never easy. However, recognizing that inevitability, we cognitively accept that reality, difficult though it may be.

Can we do anything to make this reality less painful? I think so.

It begins as we live in such relationship that there will be no regrets when the day comes that we're looking into the caskets of our loved ones—and know in the depths of our own hearts that we had left nothing unsaid that we should have said, undone that we should have done— that we are living a life that would make godly parents proud to say, "That's my daughter/son!"

Some parents live godly lives and thus give their children and grandchildren (subsequent generations) a heritage of which to be proud. (Such parents also give the preacher something positive to work with at the funeral.) Thankfully, my own mother lived that kind of life—with her husband and my father, with her children, with her friends and neighbors. And when the time came to stand before the large gathering of people whose lives had been touched by Hazel Margaret Summers Peterson, I could open the Word of God to selected and appropriate passages of Scripture and say with confidence that my mother had been a living example of those biblical principles. There is great comfort in that!

The same was true several years later when my father died. And I never cease to be amazed at the quiet, positive impact that the lives of two, simple, "country people" had on so many other people.

The phone calls came—usually during the day—from my sister Gina King. She had a growing concern for our father's health. He was always tired, and there seemed to be no improvement, even though he had been to his family doctor, Dr. Barron, numerous times. But when the phone calls were accompanied by tears brought on by the emotional drain and sincere concern of my sister, I knew that it was time for the elder son and brother to step in and do something.

I instructed Gina to make a new-patient appointment with the cardiology group that cared for David King, her husband Allan's father, who had recently recovered from open heart surgery, which one of their physicians had performed. Gina asked, "But, Dale, what about Daddy?" I responded rather matter-of-factly, "You worry about getting the appointment with the cardiologist; I'll handle Dad!"

In my subsequent phone call to Dad, I shared with him that I had instructed Gina to make an appointment for him with another doctor—a cardiologist. He initially responded, "Don't you think that's a little presumptuous?" But he clearly understood as I explained Gina's numerous phone calls, concerns, tears, and worry. "Dad," I continued, "I'm not there to see for myself how you are doing (I was living in Davisburg, Michigan, a bedroom community northwest of metropolitan Detroit), and now not only is Gina, your daughter, worried over your health, so am I."

Dad agreed that he did not want his children worrying over him and that a second opinion would be a small price to pay for the peace of mind for himself and his three children. Our brother, Dennis, who is four years my junior and six years older than Gina, also lived in the Knoxville, Tennessee, area by that time and was also concerned.

The day of the doctor's appointment arrived, and Gina, Dad, and our step-mother Reba (Dad had remarried ten years after our mother died)—armed with a series of questions that I had given Gina to ask—went to the doctor's office. Subsequent to the initial visit, the doctor ran a series of tests, from which the results would be available in several days. However, I did not wait for the results to come to me—I called for the results.

After several minutes of discussion, convincing the cardiologist that as the oldest of the three grown children and a pastor of several years experience he could tell me the details, he shared with me the sobering results of the tests. Dad was suffering from the extremely rare, incurable disease **amyloidosis;** the prognosis was not promising. I asked the cardiologist, "In your best 'guess-timate," how long do you think Dad has to live?"

"The longest on record from point of diagnosis to death," he replied somberly, "is one year, and I would estimate that Ralph has about six months."

After thanking the doctor and making arrangements with his office for Dad's follow-up appointment, I drove from Michigan to Knoxville, Tennessee, to talk to Dad. Later that day, I accompanied him to the doctor's office. In consultation with the cardiologist, we agreed that I would be the person to break this devastating news to Dad. On the day of the follow-up visit, Dad and I drove through what was once the family's dairy farm. It was now a new subdivision of homes under construction.

As we drove, Dad was slowly trying to convey all that was happening in what were once the fields where my family and neighborhood friends had played. However, I was not focused on the details that dad was sharing, but rather on the news that I would soon have to share with my father.

As we reached the highest elevation in the eighty-six-acre development, I turned my truck around in the cul-de-sac and parked facing the valley below and from which vantage point we could see what was once the family farm. As Dad slowly droned on about new streets, underground utilities, and how many lots had been sold, I interrupted and as graciously as possible said, "Dad, thanks for telling me all of these things, but I really wanted us to come up here alone because I need to talk to you about what you are going to hear at the doctor's office later today—and Dad, I think you would rather hear this from me than from a stranger." I was focused—and now so was Dad.

Over the next several minutes, through tears, I conveyed to Dad the diagnosis and the prognosis. And for a while that morning, I became my Dad's pastor—not only giving him the news that none of us would want to hear about ourselves but also suggesting that, although the doctors could be wrong and that he might out-live each of us, his children, this was a good "wake-up call." If there was anything that he wanted to do that he had not done, now was the time to do it. Was there anything that he would like to say to anyone? Now was the time to say it! Was there anywhere that he wanted to go? Now was the time to go there!

But let me interrupt myself to clarify something for the reader. I do not share these details in an effort to make myself "look good, like the *perfect son* or something of that sort," but rather to secure in the mind of each reader that the "valley" through which I have come indeed housed certain suffering and difficulty—stresses that are common to many, if not all, of us sooner or later.

But we go through more in the valleys than sorrow and suffering. There is also survival and sunshine and success—but we must first believe that those positives are indeed present in the valley and that they can be ours. My story is a living testimonial to what is available, not to a special few, but to all who will pursue the promises of an ever-present and all-powerful God who loves us.

Dad thanked me for bringing him the news of his diagnosis personally—as difficult as it was for both of us—and not leaving the task to a very kind doctor who was but a stranger to him. We sat in silence at times. We cried quietly together as we sat there in my black 1979 GMC Jimmy. I prayed with Dad and then, after another good cry together, I started the truck and drove back in silence to the house where I'd grown up as a child and teenager and where Dad and Reba still lived.

Although the details are sketchy in my mind now, I remember going back home for Thanksgiving with Dad and Reba and whoever from our extended family was available to be there. But I vividly remember the private conversation with Dad before leaving Tennessee following Thanksgiving—another tough and tearful time, as I acknowledged that if the doctors were correct that this would most likely be his last Thanksgiving and Christmas. The most difficult aspect of our conversation that day was letting Dad know that, due to a heavy schedule as the pastor of the First Baptist Church in Davisburg, Michigan, I would most likely not be home for Christmas—unless he especially wanted me to be there. Dad, in his quiet, soft-spoken manner replied, "I understand. You need to be there with them, Son."

There's another aspect of my Dad that needs to be highlighted before we go further—his dry sense of humor. In fact, in the last conversation that Dad and I shared, we were laughing together, even in the midst of adversity! You see, life isn't all sorrow and tears, although there is certainly enough sorrow to go around for each of us. There is also laughter, and it's a panacea for a lot of life's ills and pains when it is properly administered. After all, the Bible says that laughter and a merry heart "doeth good like a medicine." Even *Reader's Digest* has known that for years, and many of us grew up reading their regular column of jokes, "Laughter Is the Best Medicine."

My sister Gina had been concerned that Dad had signed his living will without clearly understanding exactly what he was signing. During our telephone conversation that addressed her concern, I asked her to fax a copy of it to me in Michigan. I intended to read and digest its contents, then call Dad and review the highlights of it with him to discern whether he really did understand each section.

As we reviewed the three sections of his living will together, I was satisfied that he understood that in the first section he had directed that there be no "heroics" to keep him alive. I was also confident that he understood that in section two, he was directing that there should be no "feeding tubes." When we came to the third section, I explained that he had directed the medical staff to keep his body hydrated. Keep in mind that this conversation has been highly focused and deadly serious.

When I asked Dad if this (hydration) was exactly what he would want the medical staff to do, he replied with his classic dry humor, "Yes, son! I'd hate to survive all that other stuff, then die of thirst!" We laughed together and I reassured Dad, "Well, Dad, your body may be dying, but obviously your spirit is still very healthy!"

Did you catch that? He had hope in his future in spite of all that! Although the outward man was perishing, the inner man was still being renewed day by day. How? Dad knew the personal peace, power, and presence of the Lord Himself! Dad trusted himself and his eternity to the hands of Jesus Christ, in whom he had believed since childhood.

That kind of hope, peace, and trust is not something for us alone—it is something that we're to share in the natural course of day-to-day life as well. Let me explain.

During the decade of the 1980s, one of the special joys of my life was teaching a high school Bible class at Paducah Christian Academy, the educational arm of the Broadway Baptist Church in Paducah, Kentucky, where I was serving as senior pastor. The class met in the mornings on Monday, Wednesday, and Friday each week.

As I arrived to teach my class one morning, one of the ladies from the front office ran out the main entrance of the school complex to catch me as I pulled into the parking lot. She informed me that an emergency call had just come into the school office for me. The mother of Nelson Shelby, a board member of the church and a dear personal friend, had just died at Lourdes Hospital.

After racing along back roads as much as possible, I arrived at the hospital, located at the intersection of Lone Oak Road and Interstate 24. When I entered the hospital room, Nelson, a large muscular man, was standing near the bedside where the now lifeless body of his mother lay. Tears quietly coursed their way down his weather-beaten cheeks.

I stepped to his side and stood there in silence—reflecting on the Friday morning a few years earlier when I had stood by the bedside of my own mother in another hospital in another city. As I remembered that morning—as all life support was methodically removed from my mother's body and her heartbeats slowed and finally stopped—I realized all over again what goes through a son's mind at such a time.

As both Nelson and I stood there weeping, he turned slightly to his right and softly spoke. "You understand, don't you, Preacher? You've been there!" Still, without saying a word, I placed my left arm around that heartbroken man's shoulders and nodded my affirmative answer. In a few minutes, we prayed together, thanking the Lord for Nelson's godly mother and the influence she had had in his life, and left the room.

Nelson Shelby and I shared with each other in the days that followed the blessing it was for each of us to have been reared by godly parents, and especially our mothers. Their influence in our lives was substantial, and we were grateful.

As a pastor for more than two decades, I've often wondered how relatives—sons, daughters, and other loved ones—cope when they do not have parents whose lives have reflected godly character qualities.

But what can you do when that has not been the case? Perhaps some readers do not have the hope, strength, and comfort that comes from knowing that their parents had lived in such a way that did not bring calming and comforting thoughts to mind. What about the person whose parents abandoned, abused, or neglected them? You may be asking yourself in quiet desperation, "Yeah, Dale. It's easy for *you to* say, but what about *me*?!"

The solution

First, we are certainly not all in the same boat in many things in life, but if we look diligently, we can all find blessings in our lives. One glaring illustration of this reality is that we owe our very lives to parents—regardless of whether we know who they are, whether they were good parents or bad, and whether they provided adequately for us or failed to meet our needs.

Without those two special people, whoever they are, none of us would have life! As elementary as that thought might be, many people often overlook or under appreciate it. Without them, none of us would have ever had a shot at life! Forget about how tough life might be for just a moment, and focus on the very fact that you have life today because of those two people.

Next, choose to believe that God has not forgotten or abandoned you. You see, my friend, you play a vital role in both your current circumstances and your future. You have choices! What a privilege! You are not trapped in your current valley—unless you *choose* to remain where you are. However, that then becomes a prison of your own making because, unless you choose to leave the valley, you're trapping yourself in the quicksand of current circumstances.

So, if you will choose to believe that God knows about you and your valley, if you will choose to believe that He cares, then you can also choose to look to Him for comfort, for solutions, and for the strength to go on.

In the midst of any problem, we're easily tempted to blame others for our dilemma or difficulty while excusing ourselves. Forget either of those excuses as viable for you. Decide *now* that you are going to face the future and look for possibilities that lead you out of the valley in which you find yourself—regardless of how you arrived in the valley. You are now responsible. You are now in the driver's seat. You are now making the decisions and choosing in which direction your life will go.

As you begin to move against the "paralysis of analysis," anticipate the day when you will look back at the valley through which you came successfully and realize that, although at times you might have felt there was no way out of your valley, you might have felt that the pain was more than you could bear, with God's strength working within, you were able to survive, to thrive, and to bless others.

Remember?

Leave a well in the valley, the dark and lonesome valley;
Others have to cross this valley, too:
And what a blessing when they find the well of joy
you've left behind;
So, leave a well in the valley you go through.

Determine within your heart and mind as you read these words that you will not waste the pain—your pain, whatever it is! Believe that at some point in the future, God can and will use you to put your arm around your Nelson Shelby and minister His grace. I assure you, days lie ahead of you—at the other end of your valley—when God will use your influence, your pain, your circumstances, and your victory to reassure and encourage someone else!

Then you will grasp in a new way what it means to "weep with those who weep." You will understand what they are experiencing, and it will break your heart as you momentarily recount the frustrations and feelings of futility. However, those tears will wash away your own self-pity as you recount the hope that you also experienced and embraced. And your compassion, patience, and understanding will influence the friend or family member whose earthly journey has taken them into the valley for a season.

But there's another insight to be gained. Those tears will become tears of joy for you as you recall your own valley—what it felt like and how God gloriously brought you through the difficult situation. You see, it really isn't so much about the *words* as it is the *heart*—others will know that you understand.

As I write this, I am in the Cannock Chase National Forest, near Birmingham, England. Only moments ago, I was on the telephone with a dear friend from Michigan who spoke of our mutual friend Cindy. Cindy's family is going through a difficult valley. Her sister is battling cancer. After she underwent a battery of tests at the Cleveland Clinic in Cleveland, Ohio, the family was given fresh hope. Hope was also ministered to Cindy through a cancer survivor whose children figure skate at the Detroit Skating Club, in Bloomfield Hills, Michigan.

Did you catch it? A cancer survivor, by her very presence and conversation, brought hope to someone else. Survivors survive, succeed, and pass on to others the hope that's necessary to survive!

Let's say that your circumstances—your valley—is the worst situation imaginable. Somewhere in this world, other people have already survived the same, or a very similar, situation. How did they do it? Inside of each of them were some common elements. They recognized where they were. They chose to believe that they could and would survive. Believing that, they anticipated finding the elements they would need to survive. They *pursued* survival, and once they knew they had survived, they looked for ways to help others survive as well.

Leave a well in the valley, the dark and lonesome valley;
Others have to cross this valley, too:
And what a blessing when they find the well of joy
you've left behind;
So, leave a well in the valley you go through.

[Dale Peterson contemplating life from the keyboard]

Scriptures on Which to Meditate

(Psalm 84:6–11 New Living Translation)

When they walk through the Valley of Weeping, it will become a place of refreshing springs, where pools of blessing collect after the rains! They will continue to grow stronger, and each of them will appear before God in Jerusalem. O LORD God Almighty, hear my prayer. Listen, O God of Israel.

(Luke 3:5 New Living Translation)

Fill in the valleys, and level the mountains and hills! Straighten the curves, and smooth out the rough places! And then all people will see the salvation sent from God.'"

3

When Our Health Breaks

I'm a healthy guy. In fact, I just finished running a four-mile trek through the Cannock Chase National Forest in Cannock, England earlier this morning. However, when you read the list of maladies and procedures that follow, you might be tempted to think "brain damage" is one that didn't even get honorable mention in the list! But I'm healthy!

Was it a heart attack I suffered on the road while traveling from Knoxville, Tennessee, to Paducah, Kentucky?

My family and I had spent the 1987 Thanksgiving holiday with my father and other family members in Knoxville, Tennessee, and were making our way west back along Interstate 40 toward Nashville. I was driving my old tour bus—a 1962 GM-4106—on this trip, in part to have some mechanical work done over the holiday at Gene's Alignment in Knoxville, and in part because it was much more comfortable for the family.

The kids were relaxing as I drove along at a leisurely speed. Charity was reading a book; Justin was playing a video game; Jordan and Joshua (our twin boys), who were two years old at the time, were playing quietly; Joy, only a few months old at the time, was being fed by her mom back in the bedroom. Life was good! We'd enjoyed a great visit with family and were now heading back for Sunday services in our church the next day.

However, as I drove westward along Interstate 40, somewhere in the vicinity of Monterey, Tennessee, I noticed that my arms seemed to feel "heavy," and my lower legs seemed to be "falling asleep." I shook my arms and hands and bounced my legs, trying to "wake" them up. But then I noticed something else—something that really began to focus my thinking—an unusual and growing pressure in the center of my chest.

After monitoring those symptoms for a few miles and while wondering if this could be heart-related and waiting on other symptoms to appear, (such as shortness of breath, pain down my left arm or in my jaw), I said to my oldest daughter, "Charity, go back to the bedroom and ask your mother to come up here."

In just a few seconds, Charity relayed the message, "Mom said that she's nursing the baby and she'll come up front when she's finished."

"Charity, go back and tell your mom that I need her up here *now*!" I responded rather sternly. A few moments later, Gina—with Joy in arm—was standing over my right shoulder, a bit bewildered as to why I would insist on disrupting Joy's noon meal time.

"I don't want you to be alarmed," I stated calmly to Gina, "but I think I'm having a heart attack."

"Well, pull over to the side of the freeway!" she blurted out. "I don't know the first thing about driving this bus, and we might crash before I could get behind the steering wheel, especially if you should pass out!"

After reassuring her that I was fine (as fine as one can be who thinks he's having a heart attack), I went over several details of a plan that I had already been working on as I monitored the symptoms, which were now intensifying. We were somewhere just east of Cookeville, and I knew that at the second Cookeville exit is a state police post. The state troopers often ate near their post at a

Shoney's restaurant. I would pull into the parking lot of Shoney's and let Gina off to run into the restaurant and ask one of the police officers to call an ambulance, while I pulled to the back of their parking area and left the bus. (At this point in the mid-to-late 1980s, few people had even heard of cell phones, let alone owned one.)

Within seconds, a Tennessee State Trooper was running toward the bus. He boarded through the open door, and asked, "Mr. Peterson, your wife said that you thought you might be having a heart attack. Is that true?"

"I don't know what else it could be," I replied.

Almost comically, the officer said, "Well, could I get you to stop exercising and sit here in this chair and try to relax then?" In trying to get relief from the increasing pressure in my chest, I had been pacing back and forth in the front of the tour bus.

After I complied, the trooper asked me if I was experiencing a few other specific symptoms, acknowledging that although he was no medical doctor, those were symptoms that he had experienced personally when he had had a heart attack. He also assured the kids and me that an ambulance should be arriving momentarily. We could hear a siren even as he spoke.

The emergency medical team arrived, secured me on the gurney, loaded me into the ambulance, and whisked away from the parking lot toward the local hospital a few miles away. Gina and the kids were kindly and quickly loaded into the State Trooper's patrol car and followed the ambulance.

After emergency personnel ran an EKG, they drew arterial blood to check enzymes and blood gases, and the emergency room physician on duty asked me several questions, I was given a rather amazing diagnosis—"exertionary chest pain compounded by hyperventilation." My instructions from the ER doctor were to cut my schedule in half for the next week and to go see my family doctor in a week to ten days.

I knew that I had done nothing to exert myself—and I'd never hyperventilated in my life. But still I knew that something wasn't quite "right." Although I spoke in the regular Sunday services the next day, I cut my schedule by 75 percent the following week and made an appointment with Dr. Kenneth Cook, my family doctor, for the very next Monday morning, nine days from the time of the incident along Interstate 40.

On Sunday evening, eight days after the episode in Tennessee and after three services for the day, I stayed back in the office to catch up on some important paperwork before heading home for the night. But as I turned out the lights and locked the door, there came the pain and the pressure sensation in the center of my chest. I rubbed my chest and climbed into my truck for the nine-mile drive home.

The irony is this—Western Baptist Hospital was located directly across the street from my church office, but did I go to emergency? No! Like so many people do, I told myself that the pain would go away. Three miles later, and with the pain worsening by the minute, I drove past Lourdes Hospital as well!

As I pulled into our family home on Mark Drive in Lone Oak (a community on the south side of Paducah, Kentucky), I knew that I was in serious trouble—but the house was completely dark! No one was at home! For a family that knew how to flip light switches *on* but seldom *off*, there was not a single light left on—total darkness!

Fearing that I might pass out before reaching the back door of the house, and not be discovered for hours, I *ran* to the door and let myself in to the house. About a half hour later, my family also returned home and found me in the living room—"break dancing" in the floor and on the furniture, trying to get relief from the now-excruciating pain.

After ensuring that the older children would take care of the younger ones, my wife quickly drove me to Lourdes Hospital. Please understand that what I am about to share is *not* the way someone should react when he or she suspects they are having a heart attack. But it *is* my story—just don't make it *yours!*

My wife wanted to drop me off at the door; instead, I said to her in a rather frustrated tone, "No, just park somewhere. I can walk in!" Could we find a parking place anywhere near the emergency room entrance? No! So we parked a quarter of a mile from the entrance and *ran* back to the door! Not the brightest move, to be sure.

Once at the door, I jerked on the handle. *Locked!* The door to a trauma center was locked—but there was a little sign that read: "Please ring bell for service." I sarcastically turned and said to Gina, "Only in Paducah, Kentucky, would they lock the door to a trauma center!" I rang the bell and waited. After several seconds, a large middle-aged nurse walked over to the interior microphone and asked, "May I help you, sir?"

Holding my hand over the center of my chest, I continued with the sarcasm: "I hope so. I think this is the BIG one, Elizabeth," a line from the old television shows *Sanford and Son* starring Red Foxx. Now a little flustered, the sweet lady buzzed us in, met us by the door, and escorted us into an examination area, giving me instructions to disrobe to the waist.

A small team of emergency room personnel quickly ran an EKG. As the "strip" was being printed, the leading cardiologist in western Kentucky, Dr. Lowell Roberts, walked into the hospital and read the EKG. The details now began to reflect the hand of God in every way! Dr. Roberts walked to the side of the gurney on which I was lying, introduced himself, acknowledged that he had read the EKG, and confirmed that I was having a heart attack.

Now watch the details.

He started to describe a "brand new drug" that had just hit the market, but I stopped and startled him when I boldly stated, "If you're talking about TPA (tissue plasminogen activator) and you want my permission to use it, let's go for it!" You see, during the previous week when I had cut my schedule by 75 percent, I had done two things in preparation for this night—although I had no idea that I was preparing for anything!

First, I had sat in the surgical waiting room for a few hours with a family from our church and "just happened" to pick up a pharmaceutical company's brochure on this latest clot-busting drug, TPA. I had read the entire brochure even though I did not begin to understand all of the terminology.

Second, unable to sleep one night, I had turned on the television in our bedroom, surfed through the channels, and "just happened" to watch a thirty-minute medical show called *Cardiology Update*, a program by doctors for doctors. That night's subject "just happened" to be a discussion about a new drug designed to dissolve blood clots quickly and arrest a myocardial infarction almost instantly—TPA.

So, Dr. Roberts was a bit surprised that his new patient had a working knowledge of the new drug. But what was even more amazing is that the Food and Drug Administration (FDA) had approved TPA for use in the general public only two weeks earlier. Even more amazing was the fact that Lourdes Hospital had received a supply of that wonder drug only two days earlier!

If I may digress for a moment, another detail warrants our attention. While the events I've just described took place in 1987 in Paducah, Kentucky, I was relaying them to a cardiac nurse one evening in Pontiac, Michigan, in 2004. She shared in the amazement of God's good hand working through these details in my life, but then she enlarged the amazement. She had worked for the pharmaceutical company and had been in Paducah, Kentucky, only a few days before my myocardial infarction (heart attack), training the medical teams at both Lourdes and Western Baptist hospitals in the administration of that wonder drug!

But let's return to the emergency room. Dr. Roberts began to give stern instructions to his medical staff. They were whisking me up to the fourth floor, where the Cardiac Care Unit (CCU) was located. Sharon Romaine, a nurse from my church, was the charge nurse that evening, and when she received a call from ER alerting her that a 37-year-old preacher was on his way up, she began giving instructions to her staff. "Get that corner unit open and ready—*my pastor* is on his way up!"

Somehow, all of the medical people in the church knew where I was heading in life—everyone seemed to know but me! In fact, one Sunday following the evening service, one of the nurses approached me while I was talking casually with a few members in the middle of the auditorium. With a voice of authority, Era Sue Lynn instructed me, "Preacher, take off your suit coat. I'm going to take your blood pressure." As I continued my conversation, she took the reading. When I asked what it was and what that reading meant, she said rather matter-of-factly that, given my schedule, the amount of coffee that I drank each day (in excess of fifty to sixty cups per day), my diet and weight, she was surprised that I had not stroked out or had a heart attack!

Now, in the CCU, it suddenly dawned on me, as I counted nineteen different medical staff members coming and going from my room, each of them highly focused on what they were doing, that this could be *serious*. Until that moment, it apparently had never entered my mind that something serious could happen to *me*! At one point during the night, when no one was in the cardiac unit with me, I started to get up from the bed to use the bathroom. A very stern nurse asked gruffly, "And where do you think *you're* going?" Feeling like a grade school boy who has just gotten into trouble with his teacher, I explained that I simply wanted to go to the bathroom, but she informed me that I wasn't going anywhere—and she was kind enough to bring me a bedpan!

The medical plan was to stabilize me, then transfer me to Western Baptist Hospital, where angioplasty—a fairly new procedure at that time—would be performed to open the one 98 percent blockage in my lower right anterior artery. The morning after I was transferred from Lourdes to Western Baptist, Dr. Lowell Roberts and his junior partner performed the angioplasty. I remember worrying about the "hot flash" that might come with the injection of the iodine into my arteries and about being awake for the heart catheterization and the angioplasty.

Apparently, everything went as planned, so the junior partner (whose name escapes me) left the operating room, leaving Dr. Roberts to monitor my response to the procedure. At some point after the procedure, the artery collapsed, and the young surgeon scrubbed again, returned to my surgical suite, and the two doctors performed a second angioplasty on the same artery. Later, they returned me to CCU.

After eating my first meal, and having received stern instructions that the medical team did not want any heroics from me—that if there were any changes, any pain, to let them know—I noticed that now-familiar pressure beginning in the center of my chest again! After debating how to word my announcement to the CCU nurse, so I wouldn't "panic" them, I acknowledged to her that I was feeling a "slight sensation" in my chest. Well, somehow that *hit* the panic button!

Not only did the nurse assigned to me begin scrambling but also she enlisted the assistance of another nurse. After administering 60mg of Demerol, which gave me no relief, they gave me another 50mg while they were getting Dr. Roberts on the phone. He must have told them to "bring out the big gun" because they were injecting Demerol into my IV until I either got relief or passed out! But somewhere between chest pain and relief or passing out came nausea! I'll spare the reader a description, but suffice it to say that the little plastic, kidney-shaped pan they gave me was too small for what I'd just eaten earlier! And God bless nurses for what they endure!

When Dr. Roberts arrived and surveyed the situation, he strolled out into the family waiting room, hands in his pockets, and informed my family that I was having another heart attack, but that I was resting comfortably. This shocked my family because he was casually explaining to them what was happening rather than personally attending to my health at that moment. Sensing their shock, he then explained that he and his staff knew where the blockage was, that the damage had already been done, and the risks were too great to open me up for any advantage that might be gained. And I'm thankful to this day for the wisdom that Dr. Roberts exercised that day. In fact, months later, during my last visit with him at his office in Paducah, just down the street from my own office, and just before my relocation back to Michigan, he told me, "Dale, at your age and general health and physical condition, you ought to be running three to five miles a day!"

By the way, when you're going through your valley, let me encourage you to keep looking for the good hand of God, working the details for your good and His glory! That might not come naturally to you, especially if you do not train yourself to look to God and trust Him with every detail of your life. So many events can happen in our lives that we do not understand when they are happening—or maybe we will never understand them in this life.

However, as we truly put our trust in the Lord, as our Savior and our Sustainer, our fears and apprehensions subside and are replaced with that "peace that passes all understanding" (Phil. 4:7). And although we might not know how things will work out at the moment, we can believe that God knows, that God understands, and that these things, indeed, all things, work together for the good of those who love God and are focused on Him and His plan for our lives (Roma. 8:28). But we'll come back to these things later in the chapter.

If heart problems were not enough in and of themselves, I began to slip into depression, a not uncommon symptom experienced by people who go through heart problems and procedures. However, my depression was exacerbated by intolerance to the blood pressure medication Tenormin. Although I will deal with the "valley of depression" in a subsequent chapter, we do need to consider it in a cursory manner at this point.

I used the ten days in the Paducah hospitals as a time of introspection. During those ten days without a phone, limited visitors, and a horribly limited diet, I had plenty of "think time," and I used it wisely—or so I'd like to think. I reflected on many things, among them what I had been doing to my body by my lifestyle, the consequences those events were to my family and friends, and frankly, how I had been going about ministry. So during that ten-day hospital stay, I developed a simple one-year game plan for ministry and made decisions about my overall approach to physical fitness.

I enrolled in the cardiac rehabilitation program at Lourdes Hospital. In fact, I did two complete sessions before I finished. I came to realize that some of the greatest people in the world work in the field of cardiology! But maybe I'm biased. And 1987 would not be my only brush with heart problems!

By the winter of 1994–95, and by that time living back in southeastern Michigan and serving as the senior pastor of First Baptist Church of Davisburg, I was about to experience more of those familiar, although distant, memories of chest pains.

My wife and I were accompanying our friends Gary and Sharon Morris and other youth workers from First Baptist Church of Davisburg on an all-night youth activity with Word of Life in lower northern Michigan. The weather was bitterly cold when we arrived at the first in a string of all-night activities. Gary and I were to run across the parking lot, secure our group's tickets for a hockey game, and distribute them to the group, who would catch up with us in a few minutes.

However, as we ran in the near-zero weather, a familiar pressure and pain came back in an unmistakable manner. The combination of cold weather and running quickly across the parking lot could have proven fatal had I not recognized the symptoms and immediately stopped running. It certainly got my attention.

The following Sunday, I queried several members of my church concerning their personal cardiologists. The next morning, I called the office of Dr. Lawrence Zgliniec, or Doctor Z, as most of his patients refer to him, and set an appointment. A few days later, following the consultation visit with Doctor Z, we agreed that we would bypass any of the standard stress tests and schedule another heart catheterization, at which time medical teams would be standing by to address whatever problems he discovered. This time the possibility of open heart surgery gripped my thoughts. Facing a heart catheterization or even another angioplasty was not that scary, but facing the possibility of having my chest cracked open was scary.

Thankfully, the two blockages that the heart cath revealed were indeed treatable with angioplasty and stents, but I had wrestled with the possibility of open heart surgery, and I was prepared in my own heart and mind that I would face the circumstance head-on and do whatever had to be done. It meant once again asking introspectively if I really trusted God with my life and all of its circumstances, or if that was something that just sounded good on Sundays from the pulpit.

Then, a year or so later, during my somewhat "annual" physical, my family doctor and dear friend, Dr. Robert Lie, of Romeo, Michigan, said, "Dale, I think it's time for us to repair those two hernias that we've been monitoring for a while now—before they get any worse and cause you problems. Well, that sounded simple enough—until I awakened following surgery and needed to get out of bed to walk to the bathroom! My word! I've never had pain like that in my life—before or since! In fact, when Dr. Lie came to my room (I think it was the next morning), I informed him that I would rather suffer another heart attack than ever go through that surgery again.

He wryly cracked, "Why do you think I wanted to do both sides at once?"

Then about a year later, it was my right knee that needed attention! And the following winter, I broke my left collar bone in a snow mobile accident. But thankfully, Dr. William (Bill) Ward and his staff were quite capable of helping mend those ailments.

Meanwhile, in the winter and spring of 2000–2001, I went through a divorce (we'll spend an entire chapter on that subject later), had to resign my pastorate of a church where I loved the people more than I'd ever loved people and felt more loved by the congregation than ever, relocated my residence, raised two teenage children, worked two different secular jobs—all while maintaining an itinerate ministry. Stress multiplied upon stress. And the stress grew.

In 2004, subsequent to an annual cardiolite stress test, my new cardiologist, Dr. Creagh Milford, of Heart Care in Waterford, Michigan, thought we should follow up with another heart cath and take whatever steps were indicated by the results. So in 2004 we added more stents in two additional coronary arteries.

Then, in 2006, a frozen shoulder demanded attention. My orthopedic friend Bill Ward recommended Dr. Joseph Samani of Auburn Hills, Michigan. Thankfully, Dr. Samani was able to do everything necessary by arthroscopic surgery, but it was a difficult surgery just the same. First, the frozen shoulder could not be manually "broken loose" and required a surgical technique to cut it loose. Furthermore, during the surgery, they discovered a bone ridge and a lot of arthritis, which had to be ground away.

But why share all of these personal stories and in such detail? I want each reader to understand that when I write about "broken health," I have a reasonable grasp of how health issues can affect us—physically, mentally, emotionally, and even spiritually.

The natural process of aging, and certainly physical maladies, can wear our bodies down. And yet, we can develop a mindset that will help us find inner strength to face the future. Although the outward man might perish, the inward man can be renewed day by day (2 Cor. 4:16). But that is a choice that each of us must make for ourselves—and sometimes we must choose inward strength multiple times in life.

My second son, Jordan, graduated from Cornell University in the spring of 2007 and then with his master's degree at New York University in 2009. Several months ago, Jordan shared with me some work that he had done on a project for one of his master's level classes. In writing on a particular subject, he had included a segment on something that he had learned from his dad growing up—something that, according to him, I always said to his siblings and him. (I always cringe when the children refer to things that I said way back when!) It was a rather simple statement, and yet rather profound, if I do say so—"Mind over matter."

When we choose—deliberately choose—to do the right things in the right way for the right reasons, we can overcome every adversity. But I have a growing concern that this is not the mindset of our culture in America today. Instead, we seem to be developing a mindset that our problems or difficulties in life are almost always someone else's fault.

Far too often Americans are playing "the blame game!" And it seems to be pervasive! Come on! Give me a break! I mean, when a grown woman buys a hot cup of coffee at a McDonald's drive-thru and then puts that cup of hot coffee between her legs, that's a prescription for pain! But even more ludicrous is that a court of law would blame McDonald's and award a huge sum of money to the plaintiff. America used to have more sense! But I digress.

Sometimes, when we're going through physical difficulties, we become worn down, worn out, and are tempted to play the "Why me?" card. Why *not me?* Where did the notion come from that I will be the exception to the rule? Physical maladies, sicknesses, and injuries are a part of life. Few, if any, of us get through life without our fair share of physical suffering. But it isn't a requirement in life for those things to shatter our lives! Even those difficulties can be for our benefit or for the benefit of others and for the glory of God. We don't always get to choose what happens *to us* in life, but we do always choose what happens *in us*.

Each time physical difficulties have come my way, I have deliberately tried to face them head-on and *grow* through them, not merely *go* through them. In every circumstance of difficulty in life, I can learn some lesson, grow in some measure, or find some opportunity in which to minister God's grace to others—if I will choose to look for those lessons and opportunities. However, if we choose to play the blame game, or choose to attend a pity-party of one, rather than look for the growth opportunities, we will not grow; we will not begin to understand ourselves, our circumstances, or the reasons for them.

But as we deliberately choose to take the high road, to look for what God is attempting to do through us and our circumstances—yes, including physical difficulties—we will soon begin to discover new growth potential in ourselves and opportunities for blessing and encouraging others who face similar situations in life. At numerous times in my role as a minister, I have walked into a hospital room, stood beside the bed of another human being, taken them by the hand and looked into their eyes as they were facing some surgical procedure, and heard them say, "You understand, don't you, Pastor Dale?" And in those moments, God brought peace to their hearts because they knew their hand was in the hand of a man who had been where they are. Together, we could choose to put our trust in God as He guided the minds, eyes, and hands of well-trained human beings who could work the miracles of modern medicine.

My friend, God wants to use you and your circumstances—yes, your physical woes included—to grow you in so many ways, and then to use your life to bless the lives of other people. But it is a personal choice. I pray that you will always take the high road.

You see, if you leave a well in the valley you're going through—others have to cross this valley, too. And what a blessing when they find the well of joy you've left behind! So, will you—today—choose to leave a well in every valley you go through?

Leave a well in the valley, the dark and lonesome valley;
Others have to cross this valley, too:
And what a blessing when they find the well of joy
you've left behind;
So, leave a well in the valley you go through.

Scriptures on Which to Meditate

(Exodus 15:26 New Living Translation)

"If you will listen carefully to the voice of the LORD your God and do what is right in his sight, obeying his commands and laws, then I will not make you suffer the diseases I sent on the Egyptians; for I am the LORD who heals you."

Psalm 30:2–3 (New Living Translation)

O LORD my God, I cried out to you for help, and you restored my health. You brought me up from the grave, O LORD. You kept me from falling into the pit of death.

Psalm 41:3 (New Living Translation)

The LORD nurses them when they are sick and eases their pain and discomfort.

Psalm 103:3–5 (New Living Translation)

He forgives all my sins and heals all my diseases. He ransoms me from death and surrounds me with love and tender mercies. He fills my life with good things. My youth is renewed like the eagle's!

Isaiah 53:5 *(New Living Translation)*

But he was wounded and crushed for our sins. He was beaten that we might have peace. He was whipped, and we were healed!

James 5:14–15 *(New Living Translation)*

Are any among you sick? They should call for the elders of the church and have them pray over them, anointing them with oil in the name of the Lord. And their prayer offered in faith will heal the sick, and the Lord will make them well. And anyone who has committed sins will be forgiven.

I Peter 2:24 *(New Living Translation)*

He personally carried away our sins in his own body on the cross so we can be dead to sin and live for what is right. You have been healed by his wounds!

4

When Depression Hits

The words you are about to read are my reflection on some of the worst days of my life—what made them so—and what made them good by the end of the day—

Ministry will always have its challenges. I knew that. My approach had almost always been "head-on." No need to skirt around the difficulties of life; just tackle them head on and deal with them. But as I continued to plow head-first into each day of ministry in Paducah, Kentucky, I had no clue that looming on the horizon of my life was a "valley" unlike any that I had ever faced before. Periodically in the past, I had been faced with discouragements, which had been relatively short-lived, but I had never met depression.

For years, I've been known for saying, "There is a storm on the horizon of your life—and it has your name on it." That statement isn't very encouraging, but it is true. Everyone's life will have some storms (or valleys). We never outgrow them. Storms are inevitable. Sometimes storms are inescapable. And sometimes they even seem insurmountable.

When my family and I moved from Lynchburg, Virginia, where I had served as one of the missions pastors on the staff of the late Dr. Jerry Falwell, to Paducah, Kentucky, in the fall of 1980, I had only success on my mind. And even after three decades, I can still hear Jerry's last prayer with me before I left Lynchburg. As we bowed to pray there in his office in the Carter Building at the old campus at 701 Thomas Road (an unlikely spot for one of America's mega-churches), Jerry prayed for my family and me and for the work to which we felt God was leading us. He included in that prayer the following words: "And Lord, I want you to work a miracle in Dale's life to confirm for him that he is doing exactly what you want him to do."

That was on a Friday afternoon. The very next morning, as I sat in my "new" office at the Broadway

Baptist Church, located on the corner of 25ᵗʰ Street and Broadway in Paducah, across the street from Western Baptist Hospital, a phone call came in for me. It was a car dealer from Mayfield, Kentucky. He wanted to know if he could meet me for a few minutes early Sunday morning. Although I did not really want to talk about automobiles before Sunday morning services, I agreed to give him a few minutes. The next morning, the gentleman arrived—late! I dramatically looked at my watch when he arrived, and stated the obvious: "You're late. Now I can only give you five minutes."

"Preacher, if you'll step outside, I have a vehicle that I would like to show you." We walked through the office and the lobby and stepped outside into the warm September sunshine. The salesman motioned with his right hand toward a two-tone fifteen-passenger Ford van.

I said, "That's a very nice van. What's the bottom line on a vehicle like that?"

"Oh, Preacher," he said, "it's yours!"

"Right!" I exclaimed. "For how much per month?"

"No," he said, "you don't understand. It's yours! It's paid for!"

"Right!" I exclaimed again. "And by whom?"

"Preacher, you're not gonna believe this, but I don't know who paid for it! All I know is that my boss sent me to Paducah yesterday to meet a third party, who counted out $15,075.35 in cash, and I drove back to Mayfield scared to death! Now, preacher, if you'll jump into the driver's seat, I have about three minutes left to show you the features of this vehicle."

I don't remember another word the car salesman said after that! All I could think of was Dr. Falwell's prayer with me in his office less than 48 hours earlier. But later that morning, I could stand and announce with confidence to that original crowd that a month earlier had averaged sixty-five in attendance that God had worked a miracle for us. Years later, I would learn that Mrs. Stella Cost, a godly widow in the congregation, had bought the vehicle. Perhaps I will tell more about Stella Cost later in the chapter.

Almost immediately, our attendance began to increase. I placed a telephone call to Dr. John Rawlings, asking him to come in the next few months to preach a revival meeting for me. My thinking was that he was well-known in that region of the country and a few hundred people would likely come each night to hear him. After all, as a young lad of six or seven years of age, I had grown up listening to Dr. John and the *Landmark Hour* on live radio each Sunday night in my hometown of Knoxville, Tennessee. But Dr. John declined my invitation and gave me the advice to preach the revival meeting myself, giving people in the area an opportunity to come during the week to hear the new "kid" preacher. (I had just turned 30 years old a few months earlier.)

I followed Dr. Rawlings's advice, preached a weeklong revival meeting, and enlisted the help of a dear friend who had been in the music ministry since Noah got off the boat (or so it seemed)—Dr. A.T. Humphries. Dr. Humphries had conducted choral clinics in churches all over America and was perhaps the favorite singer for one of my mentors, Dr. B.R. Lakin. Lakin merely tolerated most musicians in his meetings, but he always like "Humpy," as he called Dr. Humphries. But again, I digress.

The revival meeting didn't produce large crowds during that week, but it did afford us a steady stream of visitors, and we followed up on each family that visited. And each Sunday seemed to give us additional visitors as well. In those early days of the 1980s, teams of people from our church knocked on every door in the city of Paducah, as well as reaching into the community to invite people to come to our church—and they came. In fact, we reached a high attendance of more than 1500 at the church for special meetings within the first two years.

Also, within the first few months of my arrival in Paducah, I went on radio with a new program called *The Christian Walk*. With the limited equipment that we had at the time, I put together a demo tape and a packet of material and by appointment visited the general managers of the five most powerful secular radio stations in western Kentucky. Without exception, each general manager reacted the same way: they were not interested in any religious programming during drive time Monday through Friday, but they would sell me all the *Sunday* time that I wanted.

But I didn't want *Sunday* airtime, and I asked (graciously, I hope) each manager, "Why would I want that dead time?" I understood a bit about the business. After all, I'd just left one of the world's largest media ministries in Lynchburg, Virginia—*Old Time Gospel Hour*, with Jerry Falwell! But not one of those managers would budge on their adamant decision, so after accepting their decision as final, I asked each of them, "Why are you so adamantly opposed to religious programming?" Each of them basically gave the same answer in three parts: (1) all preachers do is get on the air and fight with each other; (2) the quality of their programming is terrible; and (3) they don't pay their bills."

I was embarrassed. However, after hearing the same answer at each station, I stood, apologized for the terrible reputation, and stated that I hoped there would come a time when I could live down that reputation with them. I handed each manager my demo packet, shook hands, and left. I ended up with a Sunday morning thirty-minute time slot on a small station in southern Illinois, and *The Christian Walk* was on the air! We raised enough money from the congregation, using direct mail only, to cover our equipment and air-time costs by enlisting donors to join "The Century Club"—one hundred people each giving at least $100 per year.

Within one year of the first airing of *The Christian Walk*, the general managers of the most powerful radio stations in the area—the ones who had turned me down earlier—began approaching me, asking if I was still interested in a Monday through Friday time slot in the late morning drive time. Needless to say, I jumped at the opportunity. But that now meant that I was actively involved in *all* of the pastoral duties: preparation for at least three sermons or lessons a week, meetings with boards and committees, funerals, weddings, etc.—as well as now preparing for and recording five radio shows each week. The pressure was on!

One Sunday evening, while I was dining with family and friends in a local restaurant on Joe Clifton Drive in Paducah, I was paged to the house telephone and was connected with an emergency phone call. A board member of another local church informed me of an emergency that their church was facing and their board would like to meet with me that very night.

Following my late-night meal, I met the three or four board members at another restaurant that was open 24 hours. That allowed us plenty of time to discuss whatever was on their minds. During the next hour, the men frantically poured out their emergency. Their founding pastor seemed to have abruptly loaded up his family and possessions and moved away without notice.

Following their discovery, the men also began to discover unpaid bills—several thousands of dollars worth—invoices of which they themselves were unaware. Now in panic mode, those good men blurted out, "We're going to have to close the church, but we don't want to close the school and hurt a lot of innocent families!"

Western Kentucky had seen several Christian schools come and go; the region did not need another "black eye" on the face of Christian education. However, I helped the men realize that without the foundation of a local church, they were violating one of the tenets that Baptists hold sacred. As they realized that fact, their gloom turned into despair.

With my own mind racing to formulate a viable solution, I finally suggested that the men give me thirty days to put together a plan to buy the school operation and property, a McCracken County school complex that had been closed a few years earlier during a consolidation within the school district, and all of the furnishings. At the moment I made the suggestion, the church of which I was pastor, although financially healthy, did not have adequate financial reserves to make such a purchase. However, I sensed clearly that the Lord was impressing upon my heart the solution—buy them out, salvage the struggling ACE (Accelerated Christian Education) school, and build a Christian school that would replace the old and poor reputation of failed schools in the area.

By now, you're thinking, *That's exactly what you needed, Dale—more pressure and more stress in your life!* Perhaps it's easier for those on the "outside" of our lives to see things that we on the "inside" cannot see. In retrospect, I realize that I was developing a prescription for disaster. At the time, however, I could only see that the reputation of Christian education was about to be tarnished, and I had to offer a viable solution.

The board members informed me that they didn't think they could hold on for thirty more days financially, so I also offered to pay the difference between their income and their expenses for the operation of the school for the next month—with one caveat: I would manage it all while putting together the funding for the buy-out. They agreed.

Following a bit of a nightmare of legal maneuvers to facilitate the purchase, a whirlwind of meetings with my own board and their church's board, and meetings with attorneys of both churches, the legal process was in place. With several phone calls I was able to raise the emergency funds to purchase the property outright and leave the other Baptist church with enough financial resources to pay off their indebtedness and still have reserve funds to reasonably cover any unexpected expenses. A few months later, the Metropolitan Baptist Church was dissolved. The remaining church funds were distributed to their missionaries and other charitable organizations in accordance with Internal Revenue Service guidelines for 501(c)3 organizations.

Let's review: I was the pastor of a growing church and the founder and broadcaster of a daily radio show. But it didn't end with that workload; there was more to come. Soon, we would add Family Life Services, our abortion-alternative ministry with a nationwide counseling and support service. That ministry alone demanded that I travel to other churches, presenting a one-hour media-music-and-message program to raise monthly funding to maintain the ministry. As much as forty Wednesday nights a single year, my staff and I traveled to other congregations (usually within a twelve-hour radius of Paducah, Kentucky); set up a full cadre of sound and multi-imaging equipment; performed, tore down, and reloaded the bus for what was often an all-night trip back home, sleeping in my berth while Mr.

Bennie Lynch, a wonderful retired truck driver, safely got us back home in time for the normal workday in the office. The pressure was building.

But there were other responsibilities, such as the leadership role that I filled with the Moral Majority. As I left the ministry staff with Dr. Jerry Falwell and assumed my new role as lead pastor at Broadway Baptist Church in Paducah, the Moral Majority was just being formed and getting its political legs. In fact, Dr. Falwell had offered me the presidency of the Moral Majority before I left Lynchburg in hopes that I would remain on his staff.

Since I shared many of Dr. Falwell's concerns for our nation, I was willing to work with the Kentucky Moral Majority by serving as the president and giving leadership at the state level. However, it often meant additional travel beyond everything that was already in the works. The pressure continued to build. But I was young and full of energy, and perhaps I even considered myself invincible.

On several Sundays, one of the single young businesswomen in our congregation complemented the radio show of the week, and over a period of several weeks began suggesting that I consider doing a television show as well. I liked the idea. What a great outlet for communicating our message throughout western Kentucky, southeastern Missouri, southern Illinois, and northwestern Tennessee! However, I was now struggling to raise money for a lot of things—church, school, radio, Family Life Services, Gospel Alive, Inc. (a world mission organization that continues today and through which I work). It was a struggle each month just to service the airtime costs for *The Christian Walk* in the Kentucky, Illinois, Missouri, and Tennessee markets. I just couldn't add the cost of producing and airing a weekly television show!

However, one Sunday I was stunned as that young woman excitedly approached me with "great news!" She was the program manager of one of the local television stations and had quietly been working behind the scenes with the owners and general manager of the station to secure a thirty-minute time slot for a local origination show that I would host—at no cost to me!

With no regard for the mounting financial and time pressures that were building, I jumped at the opportunity. In a matter of weeks, our television show *Up Front* aired for the first time!

Then it happened. December 1987—two heart attacks followed by a descent into depression—slowly at first—and then a nose-dive.

The heart attacks (four days apart) were not serious enough to impair me. After all, I was invincible! Following a few weeks of loosely following the instructions of Dr. Lowell Roberts, my cardiologist, I was back to all of my old habits and schedules. The only drawback seemed to be the beta-blockers, which drained me of energy. I needed every ounce of energy possible to continue to meet the demands of my daily schedule.

During a routine visit to Dr. Roberts, and after hearing me question the lack of energy, Dr. Roberts removed the regimen of the heart medication, Lopressor®, and prescribed another—Tenormin®. At first, all seemed to go quite well. But as weeks turned into months, the highly focused Dale began a rapid descent into depression. For the first time in my life, I began a desperate struggle with feelings that I'd never experienced before. And we're not talking about discouragement here; we're talking no energy, no drive, no will to function.

When the phone would ring, I panicked. I avoided people. I stayed at home as much as I possibly could. I hid in my office at the church, hoping that no one would find me. A strange "darkness" seemed to engulf me, and I came to accept it much of the time, because "out there" in the light, there were *people*—people whom I had begun to avoid.

I remember my wife saying to me on more than one occasion, "Honey, this is just not *you*! You need to snap out of this!" I remember thinking in despair, *Don't you think that if I could, I would?!*

Then came the increasingly frequent thoughts of suicide, which scared me. What would happen to my family? What a horrible circumstance that would create for my wife and children! I knew of a few families who had experienced the horrific suicide of a family member—and although their lives had gone on, a "stigma" seemed to have left them marked by the community around them.

There were days when I felt that I should call Jim Glover, an area pastor who had become a dear friend to me. Jim recognized what was going on with me; it all looked familiar to him because he had gone through a similar experience. I owe my life to that man! He would frequently just drop by unannounced. He never "preached" to me. He just quietly loved me—came along-side me—talked quietly with me—or just sat in silence with me. I remember vividly Jim's sharing how he now dealt with stress as he sensed it building from time to time. He loaded his kennel and beagle into his pick-up truck, tossed in a lawn chair and a book, tucked a can of Skoal in his jeans pocket, and drove several miles to a secluded area. After parking the truck, he turned the beagle loose, settled into his lawn chair with the book, put a pinch of Skoal between his cheek and gum, and just relaxed while reading the book and listening to the familiar barking of the beagle. Periodically, he spat!

I couldn't imagine using the Skoal. I didn't own a pick-up truck, although I was a boy from the hills of Tennessee. I didn't own a beagle (and didn't have the energy to care for one if I did own one), but I knew I needed something, and quickly.

After nearly a week in Farmington Hills, Michigan, visiting my wife's family, I flew back to Paducah. My oldest son had wanted to go with the youth group from Highland Park Baptist Church to an inner city ministry venture in downtown Chicago, so Gina and the children all stayed in the Detroit area, planning to drive back after Justin's Chicago trip.

However, this arrangement left a very depressed pastor alone in a rather large house in Paducah. I really didn't need to be alone. What was going on with me? Gina and I talked by telephone. I was fine at the beginning of the conversation and then, seemingly without warning, I'd be in tears! She offered to load the luggage for herself and the children in the car and drive home. That embarrassed me and made me feel ashamed.

"No, no—I'll be okay!" I told her. And somehow, I'd make it another day—hiding in my house and venturing out only when it was absolutely necessary. Then something happened that was simultaneously horrible, scary, and yet wonderful—at least it *became* wonderful.

One day—morning, afternoon, or evening, I don't remember—in the depths of despair and totally exhausted physically, I sat down on the steps leading to the master bedroom of our quad-level house and just sobbed. How long I cried, I don't recall. But in those hours—those dark and lonely hours—I blubbered out to God in my despair and through my tears, "Oh God, I don't know what's happening to me!"

While I do not recall all of the exact words that I used that day, I don't want ever to forget the context and general content of one of the most liberating prayers I've ever prayed. For what seemed like hours (and it might have been a few hours, for I never left the house that day), I blubbered to God, "Lord, am I having a nervous breakdown? Or have I drifted so far from you that I am backslidden and out of touch with you? Is there some hidden sin in my life of which even I am unaware?" I recall saying to my Heavenly Father in what must have been the most disjointed prayer I've ever prayed, "God, I don't know—" and then naming some horrible possibility.

And then it hit me. While there were so many things that I did not seem to know, there were a few important things that I *did* know! And I now told Him what I did know—things like, "I know that *You* know—that *You* understand—that *You* care—that *You* have the solution— that whatever is happening to me or in me could be for my good and Your glory."

After whatever period of time of praying what I did and did not know, I made one of the wisest choices of my lifetime—I would begin immediately "mega-dosing" on Psalms every morning! I determined to read and pray through twenty-five psalms each morning before ever leaving my house. And without a clue of what was about to happen, I began that reading regimen. I entered into what was to become one of the greatest experiences of my life.

In the weeks and months that followed, I systematically read through twenty-five psalms each morning. Sometimes, reading came easily and required only several minutes. At other times, reading was more laborious. I read a psalm, but my mind was elsewhere, and I had to re-read the psalm.

Sometimes, a particular verse might just "leap" from the page into my imagination, and I paused and meditated on what the verse was saying to me. Sometimes, after reading a verse that seemed special, I paused and prayed, claiming the promise that the passage reflected. Often, in such instances, I also memorized the verse.

One such verse that became one of the most precious to me was Psalm 34:6: "This poor man cried, and the Lord heard him, and saved him out of all his troubles."

Often, I wrote that day's date beside the verse in the large burgundy Bible that I had set aside just for this particular time in my life. To this day, years after the fact,

I have seldom used that "special" Bible for anything else. But it is a wonderful reminder each time I pull it off my library shelf and thumb through its pages, especially the psalms—God answered every one of those verses that became my prayer request to Him.

And therein, dear reader lies the secret!

The psalmist describes in Psalm 107:27 the scene aboard a sea-going ship in a horrific storm, saying that the mariners "were at their wits end." *Where do we go from wits end? What do we do when we don't have a clue what to do? How do we continue in life when we don't even want to continue? How can we live without something or someone in which to hope, to believe, to trust?*

Out of the darkest days of my life, I can shine a ray of hope in your direction. Read on, my friend, because in the midst of your darkest day, God can still make a way! Are you feeling that there is no one or nothing in which you can hope? Do you find yourself living without hope? I'm telling you—you *can* hope again! As the Old Testament prophet declared, "Hope thou in God!"

I discovered, during the darkest days of my life (at least to that time) that mega-dosing on Psalms brought fresh hope my way! Why? Because you and I can identify easily with the psalmist, who himself often felt discouraged, frustrated, depressed, and defeated. However, no matter how desperate David (or the other psalmists) was at the opening of a particular psalm, by the psalm's end, the psalmist had found fresh breezes of fresh hope for his future—and *you* can too.

Commit yourself to exploring the claims and promises of Scripture. Acknowledge your need for divine help, and invite Jesus Christ to forgive you and become the Director of your life. Believe that there *is* a way out of your current dilemma and that He will guide you through the valley in which you find yourself. Anticipate the steps that He directs you to take, because the steps of a good person are directed by Him (Ps. 37:23).

You, too, can realize that your biggest problems can become your best friends—by not wasting your pain. Determine now to—

Leave a well in the valley, the dark and lonesome valley;
Others have to cross this valley, too:
What a blessing when they find the well of joy you
leave behind;
So, leave a well in the valley you go through.

Scriptures on Which to Meditate

(Psalm 36:5 New Living Translation)
Your unfailing love, O LORD, is as vast as the heavens; your faithfulness reaches beyond the clouds.

(Isaiah 41:10 New Living Translation)
Don't be afraid, for I am with you. Do not be dismayed, for I am your God. I will strengthen you. I will help you. I will uphold you with my victorious right hand.

(Deuteronomy 31:8 New Living Translation)
Do not be afraid or discouraged, for the LORD is the one who goes before you. He will be with you; he will neither fail you nor forsake you."

(1 Corinthians 1:7–9 New Living Translation)
Now you have every spiritual gift you need as you eagerly wait for the return of our Lord Jesus Christ. [8]He will keep you strong right up to the end, and he will keep you free from all blame on the great day when our Lord Jesus Christ returns. [9]God will surely do this for you, for he always does just what he says, and he is

the one who invited you into this wonderful friendship with his Son, Jesus Christ our Lord.

(Psalm 34:1–8 King James Version)

I will bless the LORD at all times: his praise *shall* continually *be* in my mouth. My soul shall make her boast in the LORD: the humble shall hear *thereof,* and be glad. O magnify the LORD with me, and let us exalt his name together. I sought the LORD, and he heard me, and delivered me from all my fears. They looked unto him, and were lightened: and their faces were not ashamed. This poor man cried, and the LORD heard *him,* and saved him out of all his troubles. The angel of the LORD encampeth round about them that fear him, and delivereth them. O taste and see that the LORD *is* good: blessed *is* the man *that* trusteth in him.

5

When You Think You've Missed God's Plan

Life was great! My fiancé and I made our wedding plans, left college, and were married on August 1, 1970. We were living in a modest rental house at 501 Hickory Street on a corner lot in my home town of Knoxville, Tennessee. My wife, Gina, was a microfiche librarian at the University of Tennessee, and I was bringing my new construction company off the ground. My hobby was drag racing my 1966 Olds 442 at local drag strips. We were fun-loving newlyweds without a care in the world.

The late Dr. G.B. Vick, then pastor of the Temple Baptist Church of Detroit, had given us a list of churches in the Knoxville area. We visited several churches and finally determined to become a part of the Fountain Park Baptist Church on Inskip Road on the north side of Knoxville. We began to establish some great friendships with other young couples, such as Bill and Sheila Coffey, Bill and Rose West, and Carl and Juanita Mason. We were involved in several ministries in our church, a congregation that had seen some hard times but was then under the leadership of a new, young, and energetic pastor, and the church had begun to grow again.

The Lord was both "growing" us and using us in wonderful ways to encourage and inspire other believers. For example, after starting a youth choir, we also began working with Billy and Sheila Coffey, who lead the senior high school department. We sang in the choir. I sang bass with a quartet in the church, along with Carl Mason (lead), Elmer Brummet (tenor), and Gary Wilson, the pastor (baritone and pianist), and played the organ for church services. Yes, life was good.

One day, a phone call came from my father-in-law, Don Woodworth, who served on the pastoral staff at Temple Baptist Church in Detroit, asking me if I would consider a position on the pastoral staff of the First Baptist Church of Washington Township, Michigan. He explained that the church's pastor, the Reverend Arthur S. Kidd, had been one of the associate pastors under Dr. G.B. Vick for several years but had accepted the offer of the small Baptist church in the bedroom community northeast of metropolitan Detroit. The church was looking for a youth pastor, and my father-in-law thought I would fit the bill. After a few moments of conversation, I assured Don that I would pray about it and call him with my answer the following morning.

Although my wife and I discussed the opportunity at length, the decision ultimately was mine. Early the next morning, before I left for the construction site, my wife agreed to call her father and tell him that I just didn't think that it was "God's will." The only problem with that conclusion was that while I had discussed the possibility with my wife and had thought a lot about it, I had not truly prayed about it. How could I then claim that it was "not God's will?" From the moment she hung up the telephone, my response bothered me. It was all that I could think about that morning as I worked at completing the last few feet of a chimney on a new house off Emory Road in the community of Halls Crossroads, Tennessee. Finally, about 10:30 a.m., when I could stand it no longer, I said to my co-workers, "I have to go make a phone call" and left the job site to find a pay phone from which I could call my wife at her office.

When she answered her phone, I asked if she had contacted her dad yet. She had. "Would you call him again and ask him if he has called Art Kidd yet. If he has, simply say to him, 'I just wanted to make sure you remembered to do so,' but if he hasn't called him yet, tell him to set a date and time, and I will go to Washington Township and meet with them."

Amazingly, her father had been busy all morning and had not made the call. A few weeks later, I was speaking to an adult Bible class from the Washington Township church at their Hawaiian luau, hosted by long-time church members Jean and Jimmy Vick. The following day, I spoke to the combined junior and senior high school departments, gave a testimony in the morning worship service, and spoke in the evening service. After meeting with the church's board after the evening service, my wife and I headed toward home, leaving the results in the Lord's hands. Because I was not confident or experienced in handling decisions of that nature, I incorporated a simple plan and had committed the entire circumstance to God: If the church called me, I was going to accept the position.

A few weeks later, the chairman of the board, Mr. Roger Sparling, contacted me by phone to inform me of the church's decision. They were giving the position to another candidate. Although I experienced some momentary disappointment in being "passed over" for the position, I remembered that I had committed it to God, and I could also accept that He did not want me there.

After returning to my home in Knoxville, I got the opportunity to begin a new Sunday school department for college-aged young people. Over the next six months, we enjoyed miraculous growth as we were privileged to influence the lives of this demographic, once again demonstrating that God will use believers who will make themselves available and usable, although the benefits do not always manifest themselves immediately. Some results might not be revealed for a few years, others perhaps made manifest only in eternity.

One example of results not being revealed for a few years after the "seeds were sown" was something that happened in the life of a young student at the University of Tennessee. One evening while visiting in the home of a student at the university, I spontaneously decided that I would knock on the door of every apartment in that student's building, invite his classmates to some special event that our college/career department was hosting, and leave a small piece of literature with our contact information on it. (Although that approach was a bit novel in the early 1970s, it was much more acceptable then than it would be today.) In response to my knocking on his apartment door, one young male student answered rather abruptly. After my self-introduction and brief invitation, the annoyed young man angrily stated, "Go to hell!" and slammed the door in my face.

Always up for a challenge, I immediately began knocking again and continued knocking for several seconds until he opened the door again. When he did so, and before he could say anything further, I swiftly stuck the small piece of literature into his face and said, "If you ever change your mind, here's something with our name, address, and phone number on it." As quickly as he snatched the paper from my hand, I turned and walked away, listening to the door slam once again.

Now, let's fast-forward from the fall of 1971 to late winter-early spring of 1978. The SMITE Singers from

Liberty University (Liberty Baptist College in those days) and I were scheduled to sing and speak respectively at a large Christian school in the East Tennessee area known as the Tri-Cities—Kingsport, Johnson City, and Bristol. After such programs, it was customary for me to meet people from the audience, autograph their Bibles, and interact for a few minutes before boarding our tour buses and head for home.

For several minutes, while chatting with parents, staff, and students from the Tri-Cities Christian School, I had noticed a young couple at the back of the group of people who were crowding around to have their Bibles signed. Finally, when everyone had walked away except them, I turned to the handsome young couple and said, "You two must be the most patient people in the house tonight!" We shook hands—then the blessing began!

While shaking my hand, the young gentleman introduced himself and his new bride of only a few months. Then he said something that really captured my attention. "You don't remember me," he continued, "but I was a student at the University of Tennessee back in 1971, and you knocked on my apartment door one night and invited me to your youth group." (Although I had never known his name until that moment when he introduced himself and his beautiful wife, I remembered the incident that he was about to recount!) He continued, "I told you where to go and slammed the door in your face—and I'm embarrassed about that now—but there's something that I think you should know and that you will appreciate."

He told me how his actions toward me that night had haunted him for weeks, as did my reaction of knocking again until he answered, then inviting him to come anyway if he ever changed his mind. One Sunday morning, he decided to visit the Fountain Park Baptist Church because he had some questions about the literature that I had quickly stuck into his face. Upon his arrival at the church between services, he stood near the front entrance to the church, at the rear of the auditorium, hoping to spot me in the crowd. Billy Coffey, the senior high school youth pastor, saw the young man, approached him, introduced himself, and asked, "Is there someone that I can help you find? You seem to be looking for someone."

After Billy heard the description, he said, "Oh, you're talking about Dale Peterson! He and his family just recently moved to Michigan, but is there something with which I can help you?" The young student shared with Billy the incident at the apartment door several weeks earlier and how he had read the literature that I had stuck in his face and began to ask his questions. Within a few minutes, that young man was bowing his head and in prayer, asking Jesus Christ to become his Savior! Now, he and I were together again, but under totally different circumstances.

"Mr. Peterson, I wanted you to know that your efforts were not in vain. Thank you for being faithful, even when I was so rude to you that night. Because of your faithfulness, I accepted Christ as my own personal Savior! At the end of the next term, I transferred to Bob Jones University in Greenville, South Carolina, where we met (acknowledging his new wife). After graduating, we both came to teach here in the Christian school. And, Dale, it's all been possible because you wouldn't take 'No' for an answer at my door that night back at UT!"

Yes, back in the early 1970s life was good, and God was using my young family to influence other people for the cause of Christ. In fact, the more I was consumed with ministry opportunities, the more my young construction business got in the way, even though it was beginning to grow. In fact, I had bid on several jobs, gotten the contracts (which in those days was most often a handshake), but I was afraid. What if I had forgotten something in my bids? What if I "lost my shirt" on one of my jobs? So when a job offer to become the general foreman for a construction company in Allen Park, Michigan, was presented to me, I decided that a salary and benefits was much safer than the risks I was taking in Knoxville. We moved to Taylor, Michigan. There is something wrong with anyone who would move to Michigan in January!

After less than six months in the new construction job, I was miserable. The work itself was not difficult, but it held no gratification for me. The owner of the company, Fred Stokes, was a wonderful Christian man, and God would use him again later in my life to bless and sustain my family and me in a wonderful way. However, at wit's end with myself one afternoon while driving home from work in my company-provided van and passing Detroit's Metropolitan airport on east-bound I-94, I was praying. I assumed that I must have misunderstood God's plan for my life and was thinking only about myself and the safety of money and a job. The only thing I knew to do was go back to where I last knew that I was *in* God's plan and start over. I committed that to Him as I drove along the freeway.

Within a few minutes of that prayer, I arrived at my home on Beech-Daly Road in Taylor. As I was unlocking the door, I could hear the phone ringing, and I barely answered it before Roger Sparling could hang up. He introduced himself, not sure whether I might remember him. Then he said, "We're still interested in you if you are interested in us. By "us," he meant the board and members of the First Baptist Church of Washington, Michigan, where I had candidated a year earlier but they had hired someone else. Suddenly, I knew that God had not abandoned me or forgotten me but rather was preparing me for a new step in His plan for my life and ministry. Three weeks later, I arrived at the church to assume my new role as youth pastor under the leadership of Rev. Art Kidd, where I served for three very productive years.

Perhaps one would think that patience and trust would become lessons learned through times of doubts, frustration, or transition, but apparently that was not the case for me! As the third anniversary of joining the staff at Washington approached, I again became restless. The youth ministry at the church was booming! During the first year I was on staff, the board also asked me to take the music ministry, leading some of the best singers in the state of Michigan! Everything seemed to be going well—on the surface—but I was restless in my heart and spirit. Once again, I began to feel that I was missing God's plan for my life and ministry, and yet I could not identify anything specific.

My best friend, another youth pastor, David Brown from Southgate, Michigan, and I traveled together to a conference for pastors in Springfield, Missouri. It was hosted by Baptist Bible College, the flagship school for the Baptist Bible Fellowship International. My intention was to search for a "new job." However, once at the venue, I could not bring myself actually to go stand in front of the large display where churches looking for youth pastors and music directors was posted. Meanwhile, several missionary acquaintances jokingly said things to me like, "You know, Dale, if you would just get right with God, you could come to Mexico (or Ethiopia, or wherever they were serving at the time) and help me!"

Finally, late on Wednesday evening, I was so miserable that I could not even sleep. Rolling out of bed and onto my knees, I prayed what must have been a prayer of confusion and frustration; but those are the kinds of prayers that are contrite and that God specializes in answering! I sobbed out to God that I didn't know what was going on, what I needed to do, or where I should be doing it. I had not yet learned that "the *what* is more important than the *where!*" (That statement might seem confusing, so let me explain what I mean. If we are not doing *what* we ought to be doing right where we are at the moment, moving to some*where* else is not the solution.) I named in my prayer the missionaries (and their respective fields) who had spoken to me, even in jest, and told God that I was willing to go to work with each of them. When I had exhausted myself listing all that I was surrendering to Him, almost as an after-thought I told God that if He did not direct my steps otherwise, then I would assume that I had been "in the flesh" and would return to First Baptist Church of Washington and give everything that I had with reckless abandon. Upon climbing back into bed, I immediately fell asleep and did not awaken until the alarm went off.

Dave and I had breakfast together, but, uncharacteristically, we hardly even spoke to each other over breakfast that morning. We drove to the campus from our hotel in silence. As the two of us walked into the lobby of the field house where the open sessions were being held, Dr. Golden Blount, for whom Dave Brown worked, approached us and exuberantly exclaimed, "Dale! Dr. Tom Malone Sr. wants to talk to you."

"Well, where is he?" I asked as I looked around the lobby.

Golden, ever a prankster, replied, "Oh, he had to fly back to Pontiac, Michigan, earlier this morning, but he wants you to call him as soon as you get back to Detroit!"

Right! I thought. *This is another one of Golden's pranks!* However, he tried to assure me that Dr. Malone seriously did want me to call him. Upon my return to the Detroit area, I hesitantly made the call to the Emmanuel Baptist Church. Gertrude Lindsey (now with the Lord), the church receptionist, answered.

"Good morning, Emmanuel Baptist Church!"

When I identified myself, her response was a great relief.

"Yes! Dr. Malone is expecting your call." She transferred me to his office phone. In a brief conversation, Dr. Malone shared why he wanted to talk, and I'll never forget that deep, raspy voice as he said, "Reverend Peterson, we're looking for a youth man and just believe that you are God's man for the job."

We set an appointment for the next day, and I met with Dr. Tom Malone Sr. and Tom Malone Jr. at "Doc's" office at Midwestern Baptist College. I could hardly believe what God was doing—and He was doing it at lightning speed!

I don't recall all that we discussed in that initial meeting. However, one thing that Doc asked me has stuck with me over the years: "Reverend Peterson, what would you have to have in order to come to work with us here at Emmanuel Baptist Church?" He was asking me about the financial requirements. I had no clue what to ask for specifically, but, in retrospect, I think I gave a wise answer.

"Dr. Malone, I've never set a price tag on my ministry, but I will tell you what my current financial package is, and think you will understand that my family and I are on a budget that we would still need to meet."

Again, his unique voice and words are etched in my memory: "Well, Reverend Peterson," (everybody in ministry was either a "Reverend" or a "Doctor" to Malone!) "we will at least do *that*! How soon can you start?"

Isn't it interesting that after months of personal struggle, the Lord already had His solution to my dilemma in the works? Doesn't it make you wonder that perhaps God has a solution to your circumstance, your dilemma, your storm, or your valley as well? Perhaps rather than thinking, *Yeah, well, Dale, God might do stuff like that for you, but He never has done anything like that for me!* you could at least hope that this might be the first time He would do it for you. God would love to work in your life, but it will require that you look to Him, that you trust Him and Him alone. That means you are faced with a choice: Will you trust Him, or will you continue to look elsewhere for something or someone in which you will trust?

As I write these words, I think I understand better what King David meant when he penned the words, "I have been young, and now am old; yet have I not seen the righteous forsaken, nor his seed begging bread" (Psalm 37:25). It is with the confidence of many answered prayers and God's very present help in times of trouble that I can encourage you, trust Him. Call on Him in prayer. Ask Him to show you the way in which to walk and the thing that you are to do. (See Jeremiah 42:3.)

But let me continue, lest you think that I learned fully that lesson once for all! I assure you that I did not, and I have come to repeat it again and again, as you will see.

The ministries of the Emmanuel Baptist Church and of Dr. Tom Malone were legendary among Baptists in the United States. The church had become a mega-church before anyone had ever coined the phrase. In part, that growth was due to a large bus ministry that reached hundreds, sometimes thousands, of children and teenagers each week. However, because of the financial expenses of expanding such a ministry, the time came when cut-backs were necessary, but with the cutbacks came a drop in attendance and in morale. Soon the church was in decline. The debt increased. Cash flow slowed to a trickle in contrast to what it once had been. Sometimes not every staff member could cash his or her paycheck, especially at the college. Morale continued to decline, as did the enrollment at the school and attendance at the church. Once again, I began to struggle within myself. Had I missed God's plan for my life?

One day I stopped by the college, located only one mile from the church complex, to pick up my good friend Dr. Levy Cory, who was the vice-president of Midwestern Baptist College. Levy had some paperwork to wrap up before he could leave and said to me, "Pick up the book on my coffee table, turn to page (I've forgotten the number), and read the sentence that is underlined."

"I don't have time to play games—I'm starving. Let's go!" I retorted.

Levy insisted, "I must get these letters signed and into my secretary's hands before we can leave, so pick up the book and read the sentence on page (whatever it was)." I grabbed the book, *Confident Pastoral Leadership* by Howard F. Sugden and Warren W. Wiersbe, opened it, and quickly read a sentence that said something like this: "The Lord begins to move the heart long before he moves the man." By the time my friend had finished signing his letters, he had asked me to read that same sentence two or three times. At lunch we discussed Levy's observation of my own life and ministry, which mirrored his own concerns for the decline of our church and college.

One week, finding myself once again "at wit's end," everything seemed overwhelming. Within a five-day period, I received four phone calls—four different pastors who asked me to consider accepting a position on their staff. The first came from my long-time mentor, Dr. John Rawlings, then-pastor of the historic Landmark Baptist Temple in Cincinnati, Ohio. Having spoken for me on several occasions at youth camps and rallies, Dr. John was aware of my ministry with teenagers based in the greater Detroit area. He asked me to come to Cincinnati to coordinate an elaborate network of local church youth ministries. A second call came from Dr. Fred Brewer in Huntington, West Virginia. Fred, another long-term family friend, had recently lost his associate, Arnie Smith, who had become a missionary in Central America. Fred wanted me to accept the position that Arnie had vacated. The third call was from my own father-in-law, who asked me to pray and fast about the possibility of planting a church in a prominent community in a western suburb of Detroit.

The fourth call came from Lynchburg, Virginia. Dr. Jerry Falwell was interested in talking about expanding the missions' ministry of the Thomas Road Baptist Church, and he thought that I, alongside my friend Roscoe Brewer, brother of Fred Brewer, could help facilitate that expansion. Of course, a fifth option was to remain where I was serving in Pontiac. I was thoroughly confused. Now what should I do?

Perhaps one might think that to have five options on the table would be a wonderful problem to have, and in a sense that is true. However, such a circumstance does not bring peace but confusion. The question becomes "What do you do when you don't know what to do?"

As I pondered that very question, I came to the only logical answer—*do what you know to do*. Therefore, my response was to continue faithfully, right where I was serving, and allow God to close the doors and make plain to me what He expected me to do. ("Bloom where you're planted," Holland B London always said.) No one knew my heart better than God. He was aware of even the secret places of my heart, places that even I did not know, including my thoughts and intents. One by one, the doors closed almost as quickly as they had opened, as I prayed multiple times each day for the Lord to make plain to me exactly what He wanted me to do and where He wanted me to do His bidding.

Finally, I was left with two choices—stay in Pontiac or go to Lynchburg, Virginia. Then it was as though God "went silent," leaving me to determine on my own what I should do. I felt impressed by His Spirit to define clearly what He *wanted* me to do with my life and ministry and then discern *where* I could best accomplish that purpose. To respond accordingly to the conclusion would require relocation of my family from Michigan, which had now become "home," and my beginning ministry in a high-profile, fast-paced mega-church. The thought was simultaneously exciting and scary. Believing the move to Lynchburg would allow me to best fulfill God's direction on my life and ministry; we sold our house in Michigan— miraculously— and relocated to Virginia. The growth of my ministry now became exponential—from speaking several times each year around the eastern half of the United States to speaking and leading multiple teams of singers and other professional orientation ministry teams globally.

However, and in spite of the fact that I loved my pastoral position under Dr. Jerry Falwell, the role required almost non-stop travel within the United States and nearly thirty different foreign countries. At the zenith of the growth cycle of the mission ministry of Thomas Road Baptist Church, that department employed more than twenty-five full-time staff members who collectively were responsible for fifteen different ministry teams working both domestically and internationally each year. It was exciting, to say the least, but the logistics could be highly stressful, which I could easily handle at the ripe old age of 27, my age when I went on staff. However, there was another dimension to the stress that became problematic—I had become an absentee husband and father.

How could I reconcile my responsibilities? With passing time, the pressures increased. On the ministry side of the equation, it was exciting, though stressful. When all was progressing well, I loved it; yet the problems were demanding, and often I had little time in which to solve them. Often, I had to handle the difficulties from pay phones in airports or from hotel rooms. At times, my staff back at the office in Lynchburg could work through the difficulties; at other times, the problem waited for me to solve when I returned, which might be only for a few days before leaving town again. Yet there still remained the increasing pressure that came from within my own heart as a husband and father—someone who was not always there when important milestones in the lives of my children and wife were taking place. For example, my oldest son Justin accepted Christ on a Friday at the close of a neighborhood Five-Day Club at the home of our dear friends Donna Jean and Ed Hindson—but I received the news when I called home from the Philippines, and although I, as his father, rejoiced in Justin's decision to accept Jesus Christ personally as his Savior, I felt quite estranged from that and other momentous events.

The stress grew and the pressure mounted, and again I was left wondering, *Am I missing something here? Have I become so involved in full-time Christian service that I have left the ministry behind, especially the ministry to my own family?* Years later, Doug Achilles, one of my colleagues and dear friend, and I had a conversation about this very topic. He had left the staff a few months before our dialogue and said to me, "Dale, I had to leave full-time

Christian service to go into the ministry." While his statement was somewhat tongue-in-cheek, I understood what he was saying. Modern ministry can at times become a nightmare.

With the mounting stress came an on-going barrage of questions—the kind that keep one from going to sleep quickly at night and that awaken one numerous times during the night. "God, what do you want me to do? Surely this isn't the plan you have for your own in ministry?"

Round and round the cycle of emotional, mental, and spiritual "suffering" I could go, night after night. I began to put out "feelers" as discretely as possible; yet, that brought no relief. One night, as my wife and I lay in bed talking about the dilemma, she offered a gracious, yet piercing, observation: "Honey, what has come over you lately? You've always been the one who could say, 'We're going to trust God. He has a plan.' Now you're politicking to try to force open a new door of opportunity in ministry! Whatever happened to praying and trusting God to open the doors of His choosing and in His time?"

After she went to sleep, I remember slipping out of bed, making my way downstairs to our family room, lying on my face in the middle of the carpeted floor, and crying out to God, "Oh God! She's right! How could I fail to trust you with every detail of my life? But at this very moment, I recommit myself and ministry to you and I will cease the politicking, do my best to serve you joyfully each day in spite of problems and stresses, and trust that you know exactly what you're doing!"

Amazingly, I returned to bed and fell fast asleep until my alarm went off the next morning at 4:30 a.m., when I normally arose to have some time for personal Bible study and prayer before the staff came into the office complex for devotions at 8:00 a.m. That day was "business-as-usual," and I gave little, if any, thought to the previous stresses that had consumed my thoughts for months. A few minutes after dinner that evening, another pastoral staff member of the church, Dave Fleming, called me. His first words were, "Dale, I hope you don't mind what I just did!"

Like a smart aleck, I retorted, "Well, Dave, that depends on what you just did!"

Dave came back, "I just recommended you to a church in Paducah, Kentucky!" Somehow, in the depths of my being, I knew that God was redirecting my ministry to western Kentucky. Within minutes of the conversation with my friend and neighbor Dave Fleming, Dr. Aaron Beals, chairman of the board at Broadway Baptist Church, was on the telephone, making arrangements for me to fly to Paducah and meet with the board about becoming their senior pastor.

Do you sometimes wonder if *you* have missed God's plan for your life? Or perhaps there is no wondering about it—you are *certain* that you have done so. Where do *you* go from wit's end? What do *you* do when you don't know what to do? Let me suggest a couple of steps for your consideration.

First, if you came to your current location or ministry with confidence that you were directed there by the Lord, give it your best until He clearly directs you elsewhere. That does not imply an undue stubbornness. Sometimes we can create such a mess for ourselves and those around us that the best thing to do is to resign, reflect on what went wrong, and return to ministry another day and in another place. However, before resigning, it is wiser to assess the situation objectively before doing anything rash.

Commit yourself and your circumstances to God. Trust in Him. Believe that He knows who you are, where you are, and what has been going on that has brought confusion or frustration into your life. He knows your heart better than you yourself do. He knows better than you when you are truly ready to take the next step in His plan for your life. Let God grow your faith as you learn to trust Him at a new level. Song writer Louisa M.R. Snead understood this concept when she penned the following chorus:

Jesus, Jesus, how I trust Him!
How I've proved Him o'er and o'er!
Jesus, Jesus, precious Jesus!
Oh for grace to trust Him more!

Finally, anticipate God's blessings right where you are, and learn to be content. Is it possible that you have allowed normal difficulties in life to accumulate in your mind until your mind is overwhelmed by them? Are you battling depression? Have you lost objectivity in your current circumstances? Are you trying to make a go of it all by yourself, without the encouragement of healthy relationships with family and friends? If any of these deficits are present, take some time to reassess your situation, preferably with a wise friend—someone who knows you and your situation but who is compassionate and courageous enough to be honest with you.

Begin by considering how you arrived at your church, job, or geographic location. Did you come to your current position truly believing that you were implementing God's plan for your life? The confusion of your circumstances is not God's doing, because He is not the author of confusion. But He can certainly use your time of confusion, frustration, discouragement, or even defeat to help you grow and learn new lessons, especially to grow your faith as you learn to trust Him more. You might conclude that you have given in to fear or to greed and accepted a job or position that served *your* plan rather than *God's* plan for your life. Admit that fact to God, and then determine to return to His plan for your life. That might mean that a resignation is in order, or it could mean that the opening of a new door of opportunity is pending—that God is waiting on you to realize your dependence on Him.

Introspection is not the same as constantly second-guessing ourselves, but remember that no one knows your heart or mine as well as God does, not even *us*! The prophet Jeremiah reminds us that "The heart is deceitful above all things, and desperately wicked: who can know it?" (Jer. 17:9). However, as we humble ourselves before God, admitting to Him that we do not know our own thoughts and intents as clearly as He does, the Lord knows that moment when we are ready, when we have learned what He wanted, and he will again direct our steps. After all, "The steps of a good man are ordered by the LORD: and he delighteth in his way" (Ps. 37:23). God wants you to succeed in accomplishing His purposes through your life. He delights in you, in directing your life, and in bringing good things to pass in your life. Unfortunately, one of the great but forgotten promises of the Bible is Psalm 84:11: "For the LORD God is a sun and shield: the LORD will give grace and glory: no good thing will he withhold from them that walk uprightly" (KJV).

The logic is simple. If God has a plan for our lives (and He does), and if God expects us to fulfill this plan for our lives (and He does), and if God will hold us accountable as stewards for implementing and fulfilling this plan (and He will), then He is obligated to reveal that plan to us, to direct our steps, and to sustain us as we are committed to Him in obedience. God is not hiding His plan from you, my friend, but will reveal it at just the right time—when, in His wisdom, you are ready to receive it.

Do you believe you are ready to do with your life and resources whatever God might ask of you? Then begin where you are at this moment. As one minister friend says, "Bloom where you're planted." Determine in your own heart and mind to allow your experiences—good or bad, pleasurable or painful—to build you. And don't forget to—

Leave a well in the valley, the dark and lonesome valley;
Others have to cross this valley, too:
What a blessing when they find the well of joy
you've left behind;
So, leave a well in the valley you go through.

Scriptures on which to Meditate

(Psalm 37:23 KJV)

The steps of a good man are ordered by the LORD: and he delighteth in his way.

(Hebrews 6:10 NKJV)

For God is not unjust to forget your work and labor of love which you have sown toward His name, in that you have ministered to the saints, and do minister.

(Psalm 26:2 KJV)

Examine me, O LORD, and prove me; try my reins and my heart.

(Proverbs 3:6 KJV)

In all thy ways acknowledge him, and he shall direct thy paths.

(Proverbs 11:5 KJV)

The righteousness of the perfect shall direct his way: but the wicked shall fall by his own wickedness.

(Isaiah 45:13 KJV)

I have raised him up in righteousness, and I will direct all his ways: he shall build my city, and he shall let go my captives, not for price nor reward, saith the LORD of hosts.

(Jeremiah 10:23 KJV)

O LORD, I know that the way of man is not in himself: it is not in man that walketh to direct his steps.

(1Thesselonians 3:11 KJV)

Now God himself and our Father, and our Lord Jesus Christ, direct our way unto you.

6

When God Discomfits Us

The eagle, with which most Americans are familiar as our national symbol, is a powerful and respected bird. Vast volumes of information have been written about these majestic, territorial predators, and I will not bore the reader with undue detail, but let me set the stage for one of the most fearful, and yet glorious, methods that God uses to help mere mortals like us to mature.

In the safety of the aerie (nest) where they are hatched in the order in which the eggs were laid, the young eagles grow rapidly, gaining a pound of body weight every three to four days. When hatched, the eaglets' small bodies are covered with soft, grayish-white down, their wobbly legs are too weak to hold their weight, and their eyes are partially closed, limiting their vision. Their only protection is their parents.

The parents feed each eaglet by shredding pieces of meat from their prey with their beaks and gently coaxing their tiny chick to take a morsel. The mother will offer food again and again, eating rejected morsels herself and then tearing off another piece for the eaglet. By the eighth week, the baby eagle's appetite is enormous, and it has grown nearly as large as the parent eagles, who now spend the majority of their time hunting.

Unknown by the growing but immature eagle, the mother eagle has a long-term plan for her young child, and it does not include feeding and protecting the eaglet for the next thirty years! That bird needs to get out of the nest, learn to fly, and begin to hunt and fend for itself. And every parent reading these words understands this process; our role as parents must change from the time of our children's birth until they "leave the nest."

Back in the aerie, one day as that hungry eaglet awaits another meal from mom, he is surprised as she does a "flyover," drops no food, and, as if adding insult to injury, makes a second pass by the nest, creating a turbulence unlike the eaglet has ever experienced. He

cries for food but is apparently ignored. No food comes—
and it's lonely in that nest alone.

As days pass, the hungry bird begins to peck
around the nest for any remnants from earlier meals.
Periodically, a parent flies near the nest, food in talons,
as if taunting the offspring. And the baby bird screams
for food, teetering on the edge of the aerie, almost losing
his balance. He is losing weight now and shudders in the
cold nights because he is no longer being brooded. Not
only is his young body changing but also his disposi-
tion is morphing.

Then it happens. The female parent eagle zooms
past the nest, as if daring her young to fly, and creating
such turbulence that the young eaglet "takes the leap,"
and, riding the updraft, he is airborne, flying—or more
gliding—for the first time in his life. Oh, the exhilaration of a moment like that—a moment that is preceded
by doubts and fears! Can you imagine?

The answer to that rhetorical question is *Yes!* And
those who have taken major steps in their personal lives
can identify with the emotions that accompany both.
After all, for young eagles, approximately 40 percent of

them do not survive their first flight. No wonder they are hesitant to take that flying leap!

So, what's your point, Dale? you might be thinking.

The point is that sometimes in life, God has to discomfit us to get us to take the next step. Like little eaglets, we get comfortable in the nest where we are at a given time and give no serious thought to the expectation of further personal growth. At other times, we might find ourselves alone, cold, and hungry but fearful of taking the next necessary step to continue our personal growth process.

After studying music education in college, I returned to my hometown of Knoxville, Tennessee, and to the skilled trade of masonry work with which I was familiar. Only a few years earlier, I had been determined to leave the dirty, sweaty construction world for a vocation that would offer less mess and more money. Yet, deep inside of my very being was an inherent desire to expend my life in service for God in some capacity. However, fear of the unknown and a limited understanding of how to proceed in ministry paralyzed me, preventing advancement and growth.

As the ministry years have accrued, I've come to realize that comfort zones and fears inhibit thousands of people from becoming champions for Christ. In retrospect, I have come to realize that we must learn to move against our fears rather than running from them.

I know, I know. Some skeptical, excuse-making, procrastinating reader is thinking, *Yeah, well, Dale, it's easy for you to say, but you don't understand* my *situation!* Well, let's see.

Like a mother eagle discomfiting a comfortable and fearful eaglet, God sometime does that with his children, too, to get us out of the nest of our own comfort or fear. I know whereof I speak—experientially.

While serving in a wonderful church in Pontiac, Michigan, and teaching at the church-sponsored Bible college, I had become comfortable. My family and I enjoyed the benefits of a good salary and benefits package. We lived in a large house in a great neighborhood. I was well-respected as a youth leader and speaker and could pick and choose which requests for special speaking engagements I would accept. And although the youth departments of our church were growing exponentially and I was excitedly developing the youth ministries department at the college, it was all happening in a larger, more ominous setting—a church/ school ministry that was in decline overall.

The reality of the decline grieved all of us who served together in those days, but it was especially grievous to a few of us who believed that together, if given the latitude to make some changes in our various departments, we could not only stem the tide of decline but also reverse that decline. However, as days turned to weeks and weeks into months, the decline continued, and my own heart was bowing low with discouragement.

I was often distraught. As an associate pastor, I could not conscientiously act on my own without the requisite approval to execute actions that I was confident would help turn the tide for our church. As a professor, I had no latitude to embark on a course of action to help develop programs and grow the college without the proper authorization and with other administrative leaders on board with my ideas.

There was also an inherent fear among several of us who were quietly discussing the dilemma and possible solutions—the fear that we would be branded as "disloyal" and summarily terminated by the pastor and president of the college. In retrospect, our fears were unfounded, at least in my own experience. Nonetheless, that fear was lethal to development and growth. As fear and frustration gripped each of us, we increasingly felt lonely, our environment seemed to become cold, and we hungered to be used of God and to see Him work mightily through us.

Stop! Take a moment to reflect on the earlier illustration of the young eagle in that lonely nest, hungry, crying for food, but afraid to get out of what had been a comfortable and familiar nest. Do you see the similarity? But let's continue.

One Monday afternoon, at what seemed like the loneliest and lowest point of my life, the intercom in my office rang. (Now, before you get a picture in your mind of a large cushy office in the executive office wing—think again! My office was on the opposite side of the building from the lobby and the offices of the pastor and co-pastor, up a back stairway, and on the back side of the building complex.) It was our receptionist, Gertrude Lindsey, letting me know that I had a call from Dr. John Rawlings.

Dr. John, barely an acquaintance at the time, had been a hero of mine since my childhood, when I would listen to *The Landmark Hour* on national radio, which was broadcasted live from the Sunday evening service at the Landmark Baptist Temple in Cincinnati, Ohio. Now in my mid-twenties, I had shared platforms around the country either singing or speaking in conferences with Dr. John.

The telephone conversation was rather brief. Dr. Rawlings would be speaking that evening at the Twin Cities Baptist Church in Flint, Michigan, for then-pastor Ed Dinant, and Dr. John wanted me to drive up from Pontiac and have dinner with him. He wanted to talk to me about something. When I asked what he wanted, Dr. John retorted, "Son, who said I wanted anything?" I reasoned with that seasoned pastor, "You don't call me unless you want something from me, so what do you want?"

He chuckled and said "I want to talk to you about coming to Cincinnati and taking the helm of our youth ministry."

We had dinner, discussed in greater detail what he had in mind, and I agreed to drive from the Detroit area to the Landmark Church in a few days. Once I arrived in Dr. John's office at "the mansion" on the sprawling church campus, he reiterated his ideas and insisted on driving all over Cincinnati and northern Kentucky, visiting newly established satellite campuses as well as a couple of places, including an old nightclub, where he had plans to start additional satellite chapels out of Landmark Baptist Temple.

The offer was to come to work for him, taking the youth ministry "on the hill" (Dr. John's term for the main church/campus), and coordinating the youth ministries in each of the satellite churches. What should I do? Should I make a decision out of frustration and fear of my current ministry situation? How would I know what to do?

To further complicate the difficulty of discerning what the Lord would have me to do, the day following Dr. John's initial call, I received a phone call from Reverend Fred Brewer, who lead a growing congregation in Barboursville, West Virginia. Fred explained that his longtime trusted associate Arnie Smith had resigned the Barboursville church to begin a new ministry in Central or South America. The workload at the church demanded an almost immediate replacement of Arnie, and Fred wanted me to move to West Virginia and begin work for him as quickly as possible. What should I do? Should I continue ministry in my current Pontiac location even though it was in decline? Should I move to Cincinnati and become involved with Dr. John in a growing ministry with plans and vision for additional growth? Or should I relocate to West Virginia and work in an exciting, though much smaller, ministry?

Are you sensing a little stress entering the picture? But we aren't finished! Hang on—there's more!

Upon returning from the one-day visit with Dr. John in Cincinnati, I had a voicemail message from my father-in-law, Don Woodworth, asking me to come to Farmington Hills, Michigan, the next day. He wanted to talk to me about something very important. Not knowing what it might be, and honoring his request not to ask him any questions at that time, I made the thirty-minute drive with ten thousand thoughts racing through my mind. In short, he had made an offer on a nearly-new church building complex, and wanted me to co-pastor a church plant with him. He had made the offer to the denomination that owned this modern building complex, situated in a prime location at I-696 and Farmington Road, as a fleece. If they accepted his offer, he would accept it as a signal that God wanted him (and me) to begin this new ministry, presumably together.

Oh boy! What should I do? I assured my father-in-law, that I would pray—and pray I did, since I had no clue about what to do by this time. Stay in Pontiac? Move to West Virginia? Relocate to Cincinnati? Continue living in my comfortable home and commute to a new church plant in Farmington Hills? What a Saturday! Isn't Saturday supposed to be a day for relaxing, recreation, or at least odd jobs around the house? Why was I so confused, fearful, and frustrated? What should I do?

Sunday came and went—sort of business as usual—followed by Monday, which has always been my favorite day of the week. Whereas many people seem to dread Monday mornings, I've always viewed them as a fresh start for a fresh week—that's exciting to me. Then it happened—another phone call!

On the other end of the telephone line was Dr. Jerry Falwell. I knew *about* Dr. Falwell but did not know him personally, and he certainly didn't know me. However, he and my friend Roscoe Brewer, missions pastor at Falwell's Thomas Road Baptist Church (TRBC) in Lynchburg, Virginia, had been discussing the future growth of the missions ministry of the church and the development of the missions department of Liberty University (Liberty Baptist College at that time). He asked if I would be willing to fly to Lynchburg to talk with them about coming to TRBC as one of their associate pastors.

Are you keeping track here? Within an eight-day window, my frustrations and fears were being bombarded with great possibilities for ministry and personal growth. But would I choose to move against my fears, overcome my frustrations, and courageously choose to take the flying leap into the unknown of my future? Later in the chapter, we will come back to this concept of taking the flying leap into the unknown by trusting the promises and principles of God.

Back in the late winter or early spring, I had invited Roscoe Brewer to come to Michigan to speak at a youth rally for the Southern Michigan Youth Fellowship, a youth organization of which I was president. After he explained that he was primarily traveling with a team of singers, I agreed to have both Roscoe and the SMITE (Student Missionary Intern Training for Evangelism) Singers come for the meeting.

That evening, the auditorium was packed with teen-agers, the team was marvelous, and many young people came to put their faith in Jesus Christ as their Savior and several others surrendered their lives to serve the Lord in vocational ministry. But something from our dinner conversation that evening had resonated with Roscoe, and he invited me to fly to Lynchburg and accompany him to Mexico City in a couple of months with a chil-dren's ministry team, which I did.

During the trip, Roscoe and I spent hours discussing how we could combine our ministries for greater global impact. By the time we departed from Querétaro near Mexico City, our plan was to open four regional SMITE offices around the country that would involve thou-sands of high school and college-aged young men and women in hands-on short-term missionary experiences throughout the world. Roscoe promised to get back to me as quickly as he could bounce our plan off Dr. Falwell, for whom he worked at the time.

Rather than a call from Roscoe, I was on the phone with Dr. Falwell (whom we all called Jerry in those days), agreeing to flying to Lynchburg and hear the newly revised plan. Within a few days, my lifelong friend

David Brown, then chief financial officer for Old Time Gospel Hour, met me at the airport in Lynchburg. He gave me a thumbnail briefing on the ministries of TRBC and encouraged me to consider whatever the offer was that Jerry would pitch to me the next day.

Strangely, I don't recall the details of the meeting with Jerry, Roscoe, and Don Norman, who was the executive pastor at that time. However, I do remember telling Falwell that I would like to bring my wife back, and before I completed my sentence, being interrupted by Jerry saying, "Dale, I think you should bring your wife back so that she can see the place. And we'll pay for both of you to come back."

"Thank you, Jerry, but I'm not as interested in her seeing the place as much as I am her *feeling* the place. Many of the facilities are quite modest and not that impressive—but the spirit of this place is contagious!" Falwell laughed, slapped me on the back until my teeth rattled, and said goodbye.

Sheesh! Can life get any more confusing? What should I do? Frankly, although I wanted more than anything to do exactly what God wanted me to do, I really had no clue what that might be. And I told Him so. That's one of the beautiful aspects of a relationship with God—He can handle our honesty. After all, it's nothing for Him to see through any pretense that we have because He is a discerner of the thoughts and intents of our hearts.

But what should you do when you don't know what to do? The answer is simple—do what you *know* to do! There is no redundancy in that statement. Think about it. Get beyond the issues that cloud your thinking, and reduce the process to simple steps dealing with the "big" elements of your situation. Let me explain by continuing the story.

Flying back to Detroit from Lynchburg, my mind was exploding with thoughts. I ran various scenarios through my mind; however, they all seemed to conclude with a "but what if—?" I was suffering from a combination of the "paralysis of analysis" and the fear of "but what if—? " Do I stay where I am? Do I go to Barboursville? Cincinnati? Lynchburg? To complicate matters further, heaven seemed to turn to brass and, although I prayed, no one was listening!

After much introspection, I cleared my cloudy thinking by identifying in the "big picture" what I wanted to do with my life—and that was whatever God wanted me to do and to do it wherever God wanted me to serve Him. Rehearsing that conclusion became critical to me for one reason, if none other—I had come to Pontiac, Michigan, convinced that I was doing exactly what God wanted me to do, and the timing of it all had been nothing short of miraculous. I determined that I did not want to risk jumping too quickly and outside of God's plan for my life and concluded that if God wanted to move me, I would gladly move, but He would have to make it plain to me.

You see, my friend, if God has a plan for your life (and He does), if God expects you to perform according to that plan (and He does), if He will hold us accountable for our stewardship of the execution of that plan (and He will), then it is only reasonable that He, knowing our hearts even better than we ourselves must make His plan clear to us, in ways that we can understand the way to walk and the thing to do (Jeremiah 42:3).

Further, I simply acknowledged to God, "Lord, you know my heart. I want to do whatever you want me to do and wherever you want me to do it. All of these options at once are confusing. Close the doors that would distract me and leave open only the door that will lead me to your perfect plan for my life and my family." Then, I waited.

One by one, the doors began to close. Fred Brewer in Barboursville decided to wait on bringing in a replacement for Arnie Smith and secured the involvement of young leaders within the church. Dr. John Rawlings in Cincinnati decided to promote a young youth worker from within Landmark. The denominational leaders refused the offer Don Woodworth had made as a fleece regarding the new church plant in Farmington Hills. Those decisions, made independently of me, narrowed the decision. Do I stay where I am? Do I accept the missions pastor position in Virginia?

Still confronted by my own fear—fear of being "fired"—fear of the results of procrastination—fear of the results of acting impulsively—fear of making the wrong decision—I didn't know whether I should go or stay, and it seemed as though God was nowhere to be found! It also seemed to me that He was saying by His silence, "Make a decision, Dale!"

Some decisions are no-brainers or are inconsequential. Other decisions redirect our lives. I knew my circumstance was the latter. Finally, I compared and contrasted the two ministers and their ministries. Both Dr. Tom Malone Sr. and Dr. Jerry Falwell were great ministers, preachers, and church-builders. Both men had founded schools in which others could be trained to serve the Lord. Both men were in debt—Malone by several thousand dollars and Falwell by several million dollars. Both men were always raising money—Malone for what had already been done (past) and Falwell for what needed to be done (future). The ministry where I was serving in Pontiac was in serious decline whereas the ministry that was inviting me to join their team was growing exponentially.

I then asked myself, *Where can I best do with my life what I know God wants me to do?* Suddenly, it seemed to become a no-brainer—arise and go to Lynchburg! Was it the correct decision? Yes! Even as I write these words, the former ministry could hardly decline more, whereas the latter ministry continues growth at unprecedented rates. Both founders, now with the Lord, are men that I admire and respect to this day, and each made an eternal impact on the lives of untold thousands—perhaps millions—of people who, in turn, continue to impact their world for the cause of Christ.

So, how does all of this apply to each of us? Think—we all go though periodic times of confusion, doubt, fear, and frustration. You might not be experiencing those maladies today, but save this book—you can find hope during that dark day that lurks just around the next bend on the road of life! We all need periodic reminders to help us evaluate our lives and how we are spending them.

Sometimes life deals us a hand of circumstances that deflate and discourage us. During such times, be vulnerable with yourself and look deeply into your heart, mind, and life. Can God use your circumstances to build you, your family, and your business or ministry? Certainly, He can—and will—if you allow Him to do so. Remember, there is nothing new under the sun (Ecclesiastes 1:9). Don't forget that others have faced situations similar to those you face. Some of them faltered or perhaps even failed; others, however, overcame adversity and circumstance and succeeded. Analyze what they did and how they did.

There is no temptation that will ever come upon you that will take you down unless you allow it to do so. Don't give in to the fatigue, fear, or frustration.

Everything is possible for the person who has faith. (Mark 9:23 GN)

The question naturally follows—then how can we build our faith? How can you in your circumstance grow in your faith and do so in a manner that will carry you to new heights of success?

First of all, dare to dream! Rather than seeing "no way out" of your circumstance, replace what motivational speaker and author Zig Zeigler calls "stinkin' thinkin'" with a fresh dream. Begin by envisioning the end result that you want. Most likely nothing positive will happen until you have latched onto a fresh dream and established new goals and targets.

God is able to do far more than we would ever dare to ask or even dream of—infinitely beyond our highest prayers, desires, thoughts, or hopes. (Ephesians 3:20 TLB)

Second, if you are going to grow in your faith, it will require that you make decisions. Dreams are useless unless we decide to do something about them. The New Testament writer the apostle James, wrote:

> *You must believe and not doubt ... a double-minded man is unstable in all he does."*
> *(James 1:6, 8 GN)*

Through years of life and ministry experience, I discovered at least two things that we must do when we make a decision to do something about the dreams we dream and the goals we set. First, we must let go of perceived security. It's impossible to hold onto the past and move into the future simultaneously. And I use the term *perceived security* because, for some false reason, we're tempted to feel secure in the old nests where we were hatched and brooded and fed by others; but if we're to experience personal growth and success, we must get out of the present comfort zone and feel the exhilaration of fresh air beneath our wings! In other words, if you want to walk on water, expect to get out of the boat! The modern American Christian world is filled with those who dream dreams, but the numbers drop dramatically when it comes to the decision to let go of the past and move into the future.

Then, we can expect to encounter difficulties, delays, and detours along the journey. Although Americans are culturally an impatient lot, when it comes to our relationship with God, the development and exercise of patience is a requisite. It is often through the waiting process that we learn truly to trust God and His timing.

Further, while we're waiting on God's timing, we also get to endure hardship and problems along the trail. A Bible character who leaps from the sacred page to illustrate my point is Old Testament Israel's emancipator Moses. The leadership of Moses was discomfited by two specific kinds of difficulties as he led the children of Israel from Goshen to the threshold of the Promised Land at Kadesh-Barnea. He was bombarded by barriers—circumstances. If Moses could overcome through his circumstances, you and I can certainly succeed over ours! From the time of the Exodus from Egypt, Moses was assaulted by the incessant complaining of those whom he had freed. No water, no food, poisonous snakes—and the people were more inclined to live in the bondage of their past than to endure the difficulties of the present to secure the promises of the future.

In fact, even after Moses died and Joshua was appointed as his successor, it's as though God said, "Okay, Joshua, lead my people into the Promised Land, and by the way, there are giants in the land." Even in the Promised Land there were difficulties. That's life!

The second kind of discomfiting that Moses experienced (and you will, too) was criticism. No matter what you do, there will always be the discouraging detractors whose sole role in life seems to be to discourage us! Moses was given the gargantuan task of leading a half-million men, women, and children who had only known slavery all of their lives. They were not militarily, politically, socially, or practically well organized. But the goal was to get from the slavery of Egypt to the freedom of Canaan. No one said it would be easy, and it makes me wonder why those folks thought it would be easier than it was for them. But, then again, what makes us think that we deserve a life without negative circumstances and critics?

At the present you may be temporarily harassed by all kinds of trials. This is no accident—it happens to prove your faith, which is infinitely more valuable than gold. (1 Peter 1:6-7 The New Testament in Modern English, J.B. Phillips)

But, Dale, you're thinking, *I've had all I can take! I'm totally at a dead end in my situation.*

My friend, I can honestly tell you that I've been there, done that. However, I also can tell you that when you and I have reached our wit's end, that's where God specializes in coming through for us! If you think I'm kidding, check out Psalm 107:27, which addresses mariners who had done all that they knew how to do in their circumstance.

They reel to and fro, and stagger like a drunken man, and are at their wit's end. (Psalm 107:27 KJV)

Sometimes we just come to the end of our rope and find ourselves at wit's end. If that's where you find yourself today, then you're in great company. Others, such as the apostle Paul, have been there before you. Check out what Paul said:

At that time we were completely overwhelmed, the burden was more than we could bear, in fact we told ourselves that this was the end. Yet we now believe that we had this sense of impending disaster so that we might learn to trust, not in ourselves, but in God who can raise the dead. (2 Corinthians 1:8–9 J.B. Phillips, NT in Modern English)

The idea is that if God can raise dead people to life again—as He did Lazarus, the widow's son, and Jarius' daughter—then surely we can trust Him to bring new life to our dead-end situation for our benefit and for His glory. Abraham and Sarah were well past childbearing years, and yet they conceived Isaac. For a while, it looked as though Joseph was "finished," but literally overnight he went from a prison cell to being the number two leader of the nation. And even on the cross, it appeared to be over when the King, the Messiah for Whom Israel had hoped, was crucified and died on Friday—but Sunday was coming! God loves to turn crucifixions into resurrections because He gets the glory.

Do you find yourself living at or very near your wit's end today? Is there a step of faith that you inherently know you should take, but fear of the future is griping your heart? Are you being discomfited while living in a comfort zone—you know you should grow, but taking the next step means leaving the comfort and security of your aerie? Deep inside, are you aware that God wants you to trust Him at an unprecedented level for His purpose?

Then you must be willing to envision that new goal, determine that you will make the decisions that will take you there, trusting God—His promises—and obeying God—His principles—leaving the results with Him.

You might be thinking, *But Dale, you don't understand my hurt, my pain, my frustration, my devastation!* Perhaps I don't—but I know the One who does. He wants to help you turn your pain into gain, your tragedy into triumph. On your own, that will not happen, but with God's help, your weakness is overcome by His strength. As you trust and obey Him today, you awaken to the reality that He is an ever present help in our times of trouble and, as on old song from the early 70s stated, "He was there all the time!"

With His promises, provision, and power, you will find the strength to dig a well of refreshment for others, even at your own wit's end, if you will dogmatically determine that together you and God can make it across whatever valley you traverse today.

Leave a well in the valley, the dark and lonesome valley;
Others have to cross this valley, too:
And what a blessing when they find the well of joy
you've left behind,
So, leave a well in the valley you go through.

Scriptures on Which to Meditate

(2 Corinthians 1:9–10 NIV)

Indeed, in our hearts we felt the sentence of death. But this happened that we might not rely on ourselves but on God, who raises the dead. He has delivered us from such a deadly peril, and he will deliver us. On him we have set our hope that he will continue to deliver us.

(Romans 4:20–21 The Living Bible)

But Abraham never doubted ... he praised God for this blessing even before it happened. He was completely sure that God was able to do anything He promised.

(1 Peter 1:6–7 The New Testament in Modern English, J.B. Phillips)

At the present you may be temporarily harassed by all kinds of trials. This is no accident—it happens to prove your faith, which is infinitely more valuable than gold.

(Psalm 27:13 Good News Translation)

... am expecting the Lord to rescue me again, so that once again I will see his goodness to me ...

(Proverbs 28:26 The Living Bible)

A man is foolish to trust himself. But those who use God's wisdom are safe.

(Psalm 36:5 New Living Translation)

Your unfailing love, O LORD, is as vast as the heavens; your faithfulness reaches beyond the clouds.

(Deuteronomy 31:8 New Living Translation)

Do not be afraid or discouraged, for the LORD is the one who goes before you. He will be with you; he will neither fail you nor forsake you."

7

When A Child Is Killed

B ill and Phyllis Herald sat across the table in the small-town restaurant on Sunday evening, October 1, 2006. Bill was the pastor of the First Baptist Church of Sparta, Illinois. I had just finished speaking in his church for the third time that day. It was late, and we were tired, but I had insisted that we find a restaurant that was open in their small, southern Illinois town. Having already ordered our meals, we were chatting and relaxing—old friends from the Detroit area in the 1970s. Bill had regularly attended youth camps and youth rallies that I had lead as a young youth pastor in those days.

My cell phone alerted me to an in-coming call. Checking the caller ID, I saw that the call was from my daughter-in-law Patty. Thinking it a bit unusual that

Patty would call at that hour, I excused myself and answered my phone. As I walked away from the table, heading for the exit so I could talk without disrupting other patrons in the dining rooms, Patty asked, "Dad, where are you?"

Because I travel and speak almost every week in churches and schools somewhere in the world, her question seemed quite logical on the surface. However, something in her voice hinted that something was wrong. "I'm in Sparta, Illinois," I replied.

"Are you driving? Are you alone?"

"No, I'm sitting in a restaurant with the pastor and his wife," I replied. Then I continued with a question of my own. "Patty, what's wrong?"

Patty's husband, and my oldest son Justin, a captain in the United States Marine Corps and a career Marine, had been deployed to Iraq six months earlier. He was serving on a ten-man border transition team in Al Anbar Province. My youngest son, Joshua, a corporal in the United States Marine Corps, had also deployed with his USMC Reserve unit to Iraq only one month earlier. The late-night phone call from Patty, combined with the tone of her voice, sent my mind suddenly into warp speed trying to surmise what might have gone wrong. Clearly, *something* was wrong. I could hear it in her voice. *It must have something to do with Justin,* I thought. If it was information about Joshua, surely his mother would be making the call.

In a calm, quiet voice, Patty continued, "Dad, I'm afraid this will be a memorable night for you. Lt. Colonel Mindy Hermann just left my house." My racing heart now sank as I asked, quietly, "Patty, how did it happen?"

The father and wife of a Marine deployed in Anbar Province didn't have to say *everything* to understand each other clearly. Patty knew that I understood all too well that if a lieutenant colonel had made a visit to her house, it meant only one thing—our Marine had fallen. The preliminary, sketchy details that the officer could share with Patty at that time reflected that Justin's team and their Iraqi interpreter were moving through hostile territory in the darkness of the early morning. The team, traveling together in three Humvee's, were moving at a high rate of speed to minimize their exposure in the region.

Without warning, the driver hit something in the sand with enough force to cause a roll-over accident. In the crash, Justin's right femoral artery was severed.

In spite of every human effort possible by members of his team of Marines, it was impossible for them to save his life.

I stood numbly in the cool night air of the dimly lit southern-town parking lot. A mind that was operating at warp speed had now come to a near halt. I'm not sure I even recall the rest of the conversation with Patty. I do recall trying to get my mind back into gear and quickly sort through what actions I needed to take. Suddenly, I felt very alone. I knew that I should get back on the phone and check on each of my family members, but I couldn't seem to get my mind around the tasks at hand.

After I finished the phone conversation with Patty, I returned to the table and broke the news to my host pastor and his wife. I just couldn't seem to "get it together." Only a few minutes earlier, I had been starving; now I had no appetite at all. Bill offered to have the meals packaged to take home, but I suggested that we just eat there—only I had no desire to eat anything. As I stared into my bowl of soup and stirred it meaninglessly, my jumbled thought processes were interrupted by another incoming call—Justin's mother. She had just received the same news from two USMC officers who had come to her door in Novi, Michigan, with the worst news that a mother could ever hear.

Now my friend Bill was beside me in the parking lot, letting me know that our food had now been packaged to take home. After thanking Bill and Phyllis for their compassion and kindness, I assured them that I had no appetite at all and asked if Bill could lead me back to a neighboring town where I was staying in an apartment owned by the association office of the Southern Baptist Convention in that area.

Upon arrival there, I hurriedly packed my luggage, tossed it into my black Chevy Suburban, and expressed my deep appreciation to my host for their wonderful hospitality and comfort. Then I jumped into the driver's seat and pointed the truck toward Michigan for an all-night drive. As I covered the long miles, I tried to reach each of my children—Charity and her husband Brandon, a pastor's son, in Ann Arbor, Michigan; Jordan, then an undergraduate at Cornell University in Ithaca, New York; and my youngest daughter Joy, living at home in Michigan—to ensure that they had heard, and that they were coping as well as siblings could possibly cope. I also wondered throughout the night (and for almost

48 additional hours) where Joshua was in Iraq and if anyone in the chain of command had gotten the tragic news to him.

Once I had talked with each family member, I had the presence of mind to start contacting my closest friends. Not everyone was available, so I had to leave a few voice mail messages. But when I reached dear friends like David Stokes, pastor of Fair Oaks Church outside of Washington, D.C., they also offered to help spread the word and enlist others to begin praying immediately. David was one of the first friends to take the tragic news of Justin's death globally, thanks to the Internet and a networking of ministry friends around the world.

During the seven-hour drive to Brandon and Charity's house in Ann Arbor, where we had all agreed to gather, my cell phone did not leave my hand, except for only a few seconds. Calls began to come in from around the world. I particularly remember my buddy Bob Woosley calling from the Philippines. My memory fails to recall all of the calls that came in during the night as I drove. Friends were not only heartbroken because of the noncombat accident that had claimed the life of my career Marine but also worried about my staying awake to drive safely all night long. I still marvel to this day at how the family of God can pull together when tragedy strikes. And for every brief, two- to three-minute phone call I took, several went to voice mail. I couldn't begin to return the calls.

But let's pause here for a moment of reflection—not on *my* story, but on *yours*. After nearly forty years of ministry, I know that not everyone has an army of friends around them to offer help and comfort and prayers. A lot of people in this world have lived such that they have few, if any, true friends who care enough to get involved in their lives. Yet, the Bible has given us a very simple principle for having friends.

Solomon, the wealthy king of Old Testament times, penned wise words about friendship in Proverbs 18:14, reminding us that if we want to have friends, we must first be friendly. Sowing always precedes reaping. I've said for years that *being* a friend is more important to me than *having* a friend. As we become friends to others, we will have friends in return. Unfortunately, there are many lonely people in this world who, when tragedy knocks at the door of their lives, have few if any friends to come alongside and support them because they never bothered to be a friend to other people. That, too, is a tragedy of dynamic proportions.

The last phone call I received as I exited the freeway in Ann Arbor was from Jeff Totten. Jeff was serving as the interim pastor of my home church—First Baptist Church of White Lake. We had talked earlier during the night but had agreed that he would contact me again around 6:00 a.m. Over the next few days, Jeff became a source of great strength and assistance to my family and me. Not only was Jeff a great pastor but also has become a dear friend. Over the next few weeks, our entire extended family was overwhelmed by the comfort, concern, and authentic love expressed by friends, relatives, associates, and neighbors like Jeff.

There's a lesson for each of us in all of this. How does a family develop such a network of supporters? Surely it doesn't *just happen*; and to be sure, it does *not* just happen. Therein, perhaps, lies the lesson. If one is to reap the support of friends when traversing a valley, he or she must have already sown friendship and support to others. Perhaps the most important element in this process of giving and receiving is the motive with which we "give." If we *give to get*, then we may just short-circuit the reaping element when the time of need comes. If we have *given* simply to *receive*, we risk becoming proud in the process and disappointed or even bitter at the end of the day if we do not receive what we think we should have received. However, if we *give to get to give*, we likely will be surprised at the overwhelming support that comes our way and find ourselves being humbled by the goodness and graciousness of others—even strangers.

One such occurrence was brought to my attention at the funeral dinner that followed the military committal service for Justin at the Great Lakes National Cemetery in Holly, Michigan.

The Woodside Bible Church (formerly First Baptist Church of Pontiac) hosted a mid-afternoon lunch for our family and guests, more than 200 total participants. Because it was my home church, I knew the dozens of church members who volunteered their time and skills to facilitate the lunch. My friend and long-time member of First Baptist Church, Kim Susemiehl had been working and coordinating other workers from early in the morning of the funeral. Because the funeral procession was more than a mile long and the cemetery was several miles from the church, we were much later in returning for the meal than originally planned. Yet, Kim and her work force persevered.

[Dale Peterson – Memorial Day 2008]

As I ate my meal, pausing to speak to a number of people who stopped at the table to offer their condolences, Kim approached the table and knelt beside my chair. After expressing again her condolences, she said, "Pastor Dale, there's something else you need to know. All of the mostacolli and breadsticks were donated by your friends at the Highland House Restaurant." I sat stunned. On the tables were not only trays of food and bread sufficient to feed the 200-plus crowd but also trays of both menu items left over after everyone had eaten. How did this selfless act of generosity happen?

Two dynamics were at work. First, the grassroots of America truly responds to the needs of families who lose a loved one in the military, especially in a time of war. Regrettably, this reality is not always conveyed by the national news media. However, in the Detroit market, and especially for the Peterson family upon learning of the death of my son Justin, the local media gave due diligence and great news coverage. In fact, it is quite common at such national holidays as Memorial Day, Fourth of July, or Veterans Day for reporters to contact us asking for interviews for newspaper, radio, and television. The local media outlets have the ability and compassion to "put a face on" sacrifices made for our country.

Second, the dynamic of "reaping and sowing" is also at play. Each of the five Peterson children was raised to be friendly to others—that was just normal for them. Within the context of each child's personality, all five of the children matured with friendliness as their lifestyle. More importantly, however, they knew how to *be* friends to others as well. When we befriend others consistently throughout life, we position ourselves to have the support we need when we need it, at least when our friends know of our dilemma. People are not looking for friendly people; they're looking for friends. Our family still marvels at the outpouring of compassion and support from community, including total strangers, and friends in one of the most difficult valleys of our lives.

Although dealing with the death of a parent is traumatic, we do somewhat anticipate that a day will come when each of us must bury our parents. However, it's different when we plod through the valley of the death of a child. Death is one of the inevitabilities of life, and each of us has experienced some degree of exposure to the impact of death.

I have heard people ask, "Well, if God loves us so much, why did He let this (death of a loved one) happen?" Although we may never know specifically *why* God allows a death of a loved one, friend, or family member, we *can* know other truths in which we can find comfort, direction, and strength for the journey through the "valley of the shadow of death," as the psalmist penned (Ps. 23:4).

The Bible has a great deal to say on this subject from which many of us tend to shy away. In fact, in the King James Version of the Scriptures, the word *death* is used 372 times. In addition, the words *die, died, dies,* and *dieth* are used a combined total of 555 times. For example, 2 Samuel 14:14 says, "For we must needs die, and are as water spilt on the ground, which cannot be gathered up again; neither doth God respect any person: yet doth he devise means, that his banished be not expelled from him." (KJV)

So, let me ask a couple of rhetorical questions that deserve our consideration, especially for people who profess faith in Jesus Christ as their personal savior.

- How are we who know the Lord to feel about this business of dying?

- How are we to act and react when the death angel comes into our houses?
- Does God make any provision for us when we face this inevitable reality of life?

Let me assure you—God knows about death and sorrow; but He also knows about resurrection and comfort!

Let me share a few thoughts—advice if you will—regarding losing someone close. (I really dislike that term—losing someone. You haven't really *lost* someone when you know right where they are!)

First, we should accept the reality of death. For many people, the natural tendency seems to be denial. However, it isn't until we *let go* that we can truly *resume living* ourselves. "For this God is our God for ever and ever: *he will be our guide even unto death*" the psalmist wrote in Psalm 48:14 (KJV).

Second, we should accept our own feelings. A wide range of feelings can overcome us during times of grief—sadness, anger, helplessness, fear, guilt, loneliness, and even frustration. Tears are a healthful part of the grief process for each of us when our loved ones die. In the weeks, months, and even years following the death of someone close to us, feelings of loss and sadness may recur, especially during times that were especially meaningful in our relationship with the deceased, such as holidays, birthdays, graduations, and other special days. Suppressing or pushing back those feelings only makes them come back with greater intensity and impact. Rather than suppressing our feelings, we should embrace them and face them head-on. Doing so also will help us forge new relationships with others who suffer. Dealing effectively with our own grief helps us to become wounded healers of others—in other words, we "dig a well in the valley" we go through.

A third step that we should take upon learning of the death of a loved one is to draw upon our faith for consolation. The apostle Paul wrote to the believers at Thessalonica that he did not want them to sorrow in the same way that those without faith in Jesus Christ grieved. The distinction between those two "groups" that Paul identified was this—hope. His message of encouragement could be found in this—believers have a hope that is unfounded or nonexistent with unbelievers. The hope of which Paul speaks is not merely a "hope-so" idea, but rather well-founded, well-grounded expectation toward the future, and it was founded in scripture.

"But I would not have you to be ignorant, brethren, concerning them which are asleep, that ye sorrow not, even as others which have no hope." (1 Thes. 4:13)

Death is certainly an event and time in our lives when our faith is tested. During these confrontations with death, it is important for us to examine our feelings and not ignore them. Being in touch with our feelings and questions during these times of grief and stress can assist our spiritual growth. Will we become angry or bitter toward God for some perceived injustice? To be sure, there are people who choose this avenue. This is nothing new.

"Thus saith the Lord; A voice was heard in Ramah, lamentation, and bitter weeping; Rahel weeping for her children refused to be comforted for her children . . ." (Jer. 31:15).

Will we become disappointed in God? Another option is deliberately to choose to trust Him. Can we trust Him for His will, for consolation in our grief, and for care and sustenance? Plenty of biblical admonition exists that this is the correct avenue, although at times it might be difficult. (At the end of this chapter are numerous verses on which the reader may meditate and find hope and strength.)

Finally, we should treasure all of our relationships. Realizing the brevity of life, each of us should understand that death makes life all the more precious for those of us who are alive and remain. Grasping the abruptness of death, we should learn to cherish every relationship we have, especially with our close friends, relatives, associates, and neighbors. It is important that we not allow unimportant things or people to rob us of enjoying the most important people and things in our lives daily. Make life count each day.

Again, Paul admonished his readers at Ephesus to redeem the time (Eph. 5:16). When he wrote to his fellow believers at Colossae, he put it this way: "Walk in wisdom toward them that are without, redeeming the time" (Col. 4:5).

Justin was a Christian—a Christ follower. I remember well the phone conversation five-year-old Justin and I had while I was traveling in the Philippines in 1978. I had called my Lynchburg, Virginia, home to check on my family about dinner time (Eastern Time zone). He described for me how, on the closing day of a five-day Bible club at the home of our dear friends, Donna Jean and Ed Hindson, he had accepted Christ as his personal Savior. Although Justin ate, drank, and slept the Marine Corps, the foundation of his life had been built on his personal relationship with Jesus Christ as Savior. He was raising his children in the same vein. He knew the importance of that personal relationship.

But let me ask you a personal question. On what foundation is *your* life built? When your loved ones die, in what belief system do you find authentic comfort and hope for the future? As for me, I have chosen a biblical worldview, and on that basis I find an eternal hope. In fact, I frequently made a common statement to friends who came to the visitation and funeral for Justin: "Our indescribable pain has been tempered by a justifiable pride in our Marine as well as an eternal hope." On the authority of God's Holy Word—the Bible—I have the hope of seeing my son once again in that place called heaven, where there will be no more heartache, pain, or suffering.

The skeptic cannot share that kind of hope or the inherent peace that comes from a faith founded in the Word of God and the promises therein. Neither the atheist nor the agnostic can offer authentic hope for the grieving heart of the parents who stand beside the casket of their child. The doubting Thomas is tormented continually by his doubts until he accepts the promises of the Prince of Peace and the God of all comfort—which are found exclusively in the Holy Bible.

Given that the road of life winds through numerous valleys—events and experiences that will test every element of our character—why would anyone choose to trust anything or anyone other than the God who made us?

Recently, I purchased a small, three-drawer cabinet to assemble and install in my closet. After pulling all of the pieces from the original carton and locating the instruction booklet, I assembled and installed the cabinet. I then filed the booklet for future reference. Although it's a relatively small booklet, it contains important information, such as a list of all of the parts, contact information for reaching the maker, and suggestions for using the cabinet in a way consistent with its purpose. That, my friend, is what the Bible is to humanity—the owner's manual. In its pages we discover our purpose, assembly instructions for constructing a fulfilled, meaningful life, and recommendations for fixing things that go wrong—troubleshooting, if you will.

Life can be quite complex, especially in times of grief and stress. Are you trying to assemble a life without the benefit of the valuable instructions that your Maker has given? When things "break" in life, will you be able to reach your "manufacturer," who can enable you to make repairs and keep going? You can do so through a personal relationship with Jesus Christ, made known through the Holy Bible, and discover the direction, energy, and resolve to forge your way through any valley through which the journey of life takes you. And as you progress, you will be positioned to

Leave a well in the valley, the dark and lonesome valley;
Others have to cross this valley, too:
What a blessing when they find the well of joy
you've left behind
So, leave a well in the valley you go through.

Scriptures on Which to Meditate

(Ps. 116:15 NCV)

The death of one that belongs to the LORD is precious in his sight.

(Rev. 21:3b–4 NCV)

God himself will be with them and will be their God. ⁴He will wipe away every tear from their eyes, and there will be no more death, sadness, crying, or pain, because all the old ways are gone."

(1 Thess. 4:13-14 NCV)

And now, brothers and sisters, I want you to know what will happen to the Christians who have died so you will not be full of sorrow like people who have no hope. ¹⁴For since we believe that Jesus died and was raised to life again, we also believe that when Jesus comes, God will bring back with Jesus all the Christians who have died. ¹⁵I can tell you this directly from the Lord: We who are still living when the Lord returns will not rise to meet him ahead of those who are in their graves. ¹⁶For the Lord himself will come down from heaven

with a commanding shout, with the call of the arch-
angel, and with the trumpet call of God. First, all the
Christians who have died will rise from their graves.
[17]Then, together with them, we who are still alive and
remain on the earth will be caught up in the clouds to
meet the Lord in the air and remain with him forever.
[18]So comfort and encourage each other with these words.

8

When A Marriage Falls Apart

The summer heat of June in Michigan was climbing. It was Saturday morning, and I had driven down to my office at the church to tie up some loose ends for the three services of the next day at the First Baptist Church of Davisburg, Michigan. Crossing the large lobby between the auditorium and the office complex, I was met by my wife of nearly thirty years.

"I just wanted you to know that I'm taking the kids and going to my mom's," she said rather casually.

"Oh, okay," I replied. "What's the plan for dinner? Are we eating with your parents or are we meeting at a restaurant somewhere?" I continued unsuspectingly.

"No, you don't understand. I'm taking the kids and I'm leaving you."

Suddenly my world stopped, much like in the Alan Jackson song, written about September 11, 2001, "Where Were You When the World Stopped Turning?" I couldn't believe my ears. Although time seemed to stand still, my mind was racing a mile a minute.

But let me interrupt myself at this point and run this disclaimer. Although I have been quite transparent with many details of my life for the purpose of conveying enough information for the reader to identify with the valleys through which I have traversed, I will not convey in this chapter details beyond those absolutely essential to making a basic, simple connection with my readers. Neither do I intend to convey such detail as to embarrass my former spouse, children, extended family, or friends. To stumble through this particular valley, especially as a minister, is embarrassing enough for everyone close to our family, and I certainly do not want to increase that agony. The past is exactly that—the past. Properly dealt with, the past—even a hurtful and traumatic past—can become a building block for the rest of our lives, and that is my intention.

My wife continued, "I suggest that we both go back to the house and sit down with the children and tell them." We stood there awkwardly in the middle of the empty church lobby.

I remember looking into her eyes and mumbling, "I can't even imagine being a part of a conversation like this! No—if this is what you want to do, then *you* tell them by yourself—but tell them that their dad didn't want any part of this kind of conversation."

How that conversation between our three youngest children—twin boys 15 years of age and our youngest daughter, who was not quite 13 years old—went, I do not know. I never asked. In fact, I have thought of many questions but have never allowed them to cross my lips in the presence of my children. They were under enough pressure without their father interrogating them, subtly or otherwise. But while the children and their mother were talking and packing, I was locked in my office—weeping. No, sobbing—and attempting to pray. But sometimes in our lives—certainly when we are plunged into a valley—words will not form into a prayer.

Yet, perhaps those are the very times when we pray most clearly and sincerely to God—when mere words fail us. The desperation of our hearts drains like a river of tears from our eyes and the Holy Spirit carries the groaning of our very being as our prayer language to the ears of our Lord Jesus Christ, who intercedes for us with the Heavenly Father.

That was my prayer that Saturday morning—the day after school had ended for that school year. I remained in my office, trying to sort out the next step. What should I do? What should I say? Where should I go? What about the kids? How are they dealing with this horrific news? The activity for the rest of that day and evening totally escapes me—with one exception.

Within an hour of receiving the most devastating news imaginable, I placed a telephone call to my pastor friend Reverend Terry Rudd, pastor of the First Baptist Church of Pontiac, Michigan. Terry Rudd, the late-Reverend Terry Walker (pastor of the Shepherd Fellowship Church in Waterford, Michigan), and I had met on the first Wednesday of each month as a three-man accountability team for several years.

My phone call was brief and to the point. "Terry, I need to meet with you, face-to-face, *now*! My wife has taken the kids and left me! And I need you to give me some guidance and counsel so that I don't do something really stupid as we work through this."

Within an hour of that telephone conversation, Rudd and I were sitting across from each other at the Big Boy restaurant in Clarkston.

Over time, I have forgotten the details of that conversation, but I haven't forgotten that my friend was there for me "when the world stopped turning" that Saturday morning. I do recall telling Terry Rudd, "We need to take this accountability thing to a whole new level." I didn't trust myself even to know what to do or say, but I did know that I was willing to trust my pastor friend to help usher me through "the valley" that was looming before me, threatening to "swallow me whole," and that I was impotent to stop what was happening.

As I mentioned earlier, the rest of that Saturday is little more than a dense fog now, obscuring everything from my sight. And yet, Sunday morning found me in my office long before the first congregants began to arrive. Sundays were a very busy flurry of people and events, so on the surface, life seemed quite normal to everyone else, but inside of *me*, nothing was normal. When parishioners asked, I simply responded that my wife and kids were spending the weekend at Grandma's house. Somehow, apparently, I made it through the three services of the day and, as far as I know, no one even suspected that the pastor's life was falling apart—something akin to a building imploding.

It's interesting, isn't it, that we Christians move within our own ranks, at times functioning outwardly as though we hadn't a care in the world, while simultaneously aching beyond description on the inside. At times, I've viewed this situation as hypocritical—and perhaps for some of us, at times, it really *is* hypocritical. However, when our "mind is stayed on Thee," we have a peace that, indeed, passes all understanding, even in the midst of the storm. Ray Boltz's song "The Anchor Holds" captures and conveys this peace quite clearly.

I have journeyed through the long dark night out on
the open sea
By faith alone, sight unknown—and yet his eyes
were watching me
CHORUS
The anchor holds—though the ship is battered
The anchor holds—though the sails are torn
I have fallen on my knees as I faced the raging seas
The anchor holds—in spite of the storm

*I've had visions — I've had dreams — I've even held
them in my hand
But I never knew they would slip right through —
Like they were only grains of sand*

*I have been young, but I am older now
And there has been beauty these eyes have seen
But it was in the night, through the storms of my life
Oh that's where God proved his love to me*

*The anchor holds — though the ship is battered
The anchor holds — though the sails are torn
I have fallen on my knees as I faced the raging seas
The anchor holds — in spite of the storm*

Perhaps you are going through a valley of some sort at this very minute, feeling as though there is no way out; that no viable options exist; and that no one knows, cares, or understands what you're experiencing. Friend, there is One who cares for you — but you must believe that He is, and that He is a rewarder of those who seek Him (Heb. 11:6).Believe me, based on personal experiences, trusting Him is the ultimate experience in surviving your storm or valley, in maintaining your sanity, and in succeeding by *growing* through—not merely *going* through—this terrible time.

Although my wife and I had confronted some difficulties in recent months, we had been working with a Christian counselor—one of the best in the state of Michigan—for several months. Sometimes I felt as though we were making good progress and that things were improving in our marriage. Yet, at other times I felt as though, in spite of the best of intentions, we were merely going through the motions rather mechanically. And although I was troubled by the "lack of heart" that seemed (to me) evident in my partner, I still held onto a hope that we would weather this unprecedented storm. But those hopes were all but dashed to pieces after that Saturday announcement: "I'm taking the kids and going to my mom's."

Days soon turned to weeks, and weeks to months, but there was not even an overture toward me that gave hope of the marriage surviving. Rather, I was confronted soon with the threat of "papers being filed." Although I had tried to encourage several church members through the years as they went through divorces, suddenly I was confronted with my own ignorance of the divorce process. *What does it really mean to be "served" with divorce papers?* I asked myself. What were the legal ramifications of my being "served?" I didn't have an attorney. I didn't even *know* a divorce attorney. I was scared. In fact, I was so frightened by the threat of being "served" that with the help of a precious couple in my congregation—a couple who knew the pain of divorce—I took my tour bus and checked into an area campground, lest the policeman or deputy sheriff with the responsibility of serving the lawsuit papers would find me and fulfill his or her responsibility before I could retain a lawyer to represent me. The only human beings who knew where I was hiding were a wonderful couple from church, Dean and Sue Camden. In the months that followed, they never left me for long, and without their emotional encouragement and practical help, I'm not sure how I would have survived what was to come.

Again, I turned to a member of my congregation who knew something about the valley through which I was passing—Mr. Gary Cannon, a Christian businessman who owned a real estate appraisal company. At the restaurant where we met for lunch one day, I confided in him and asked if he could recommend a good divorce attorney. After asking me a series of questions, Gary was satisfied that I was not the one who wanted the divorce, and he recommended his own highly qualified attorney from Clarkston, Michigan. When I contacted the office staff of the Honorable Robert Kostin, I was surprised to learn that they not only were expecting my call but also that $2000 had already been paid to their office as a retainer. Gary Cannon had helped me not only by giving his recommendation but also practically and financially. I certainly didn't have extra cash.

After setting the appointment for our consultation, I retreated once again to my hide-away in the bus, parked safely at my undisclosed camp site at Pontiac Lake Recreational Area. I worried about the events that lurked in the darkness of the valley ahead of me. I also worried about the depression of years past returning. However, each night my master plumber friend Dean Camden showed up, brought groceries, cooked dinner over an open fire in the fire-pit at the camp site, and did his best to encourage me and calm my fears.

On the day of the appointment with my attorney, I made my way into downtown Clarkston and nervously approached the receptionist, who welcomed me warmly, gave me paperwork to review and complete, and ushered me into an office where I could work privately until Mr. Kostin was free to see me.

A tall, well-dressed gentleman entered the office just as I completed the forms and introduced himself. "Hi, Reverend Peterson. I'm Bob Kostin! Let's go upstairs where we can talk without being overheard by anyone."

This whole proceeding seemed surreal to me, but nothing affected me as much as Bob Kostin did after hearing my "story." He asked, "Reverend, I need to ask you two questions. First, do you want to remain single for the rest of your life? Second, do you want to go through this process once or twice?"

I was bewildered and blurted out, "Well, in response to the first question, no, I don't want to go through life alone. I want my wife back! And in response to your second question, I don't want to go through this once, let alone twice!"

Bob explained that the circumstances were beyond my control and that because my spouse had filed some kind of complaint with the court, I would be going through the legal process. He then assured me that it was advisable to let the court officer serve the papers to me as soon as possible. He instructed me to get those papers to his office as soon as I could. After he reviewed them, he would contact me for another appointment. Relieved that my attorney was not bothered by the process, I found a small degree of confidence glimmering in my "foggy valley."

On the way to the parsonage for the first time in several days, I arranged with my friends Dean and Sue to take me back to the campground to retrieve my motor home, which we did later that evening. They were anxious to hear how my visit with the lawyer had gone and what the plan was for proceeding. I also made a phone call to the police officer who had been trying to reach me and agreed with him on a time when he could bring the legal paperwork to my house and "serve me" that very day—a Friday afternoon. Interestingly, although I still had no clue what the future held, my fear of being served had subsided because of the reassuring words of my attorney.

What reduced my fear factor? What changed me from worrying about being served to confidently making an appointment to receive them?

If you're thinking that it was the reassuring words of my attorney, you are correct! So let me ask a follow-up question. When you and I go through those uncertain storms and valleys of life and we are fearful and afraid, why are we so slow to turn to the greatest Advocate of all (Jesus Christ) and allow His words to calm our fears? "For . . . we have an Advocate with the Father, Jesus Christ the Righteous" (1 John 2:1). He's the One with a track record of calming stormy seas with the wave of His hand and the words of His mouth! My friend, there's a storm on the horizon of your life that has your name written on it! You will not get from where you are today to the end of the road of life without experiencing storms and going through valleys. You might not need this today, but when the winds howl and the rains beat upon your house, you *will* need this kind of foundation.

I remember that Friday afternoon vividly. My three youngest children were back at our home in Davisburg for the weekend, and when the officer of the court, a Farmington Hills policeman, knocked at the door, they were worried, became extremely quiet, and quickly ducked into their respective bedrooms. The officer introduced himself and apologized for having to deliver what he knew was "bad news." I reassured him that I fully understood that he was simply doing his job, thanked him for his service to the community, and said goodbye. Immediately, three teenagers reappeared in the living room with obvious concern in their voices and on their faces. To comfort them, I told them not to worry about the legal papers; by the next afternoon I would have read and digested them myself, and we would all sit down around the dining room table on Saturday afternoon and go over every sentence together.

The details of Friday evening and Saturday morning are a blur, but I'm confident that it included three kids "sleeping in." (After all, they were teenagers! My youngest daughter would turn thirteen in just a few weeks.) Most likely, one event that would have been normal for our busy family was lunch at a local restaurant—probably Duggan's in Clarkston, where I often ate a large salad for lunch. But about mid-afternoon, the four of us sat together around the dining room table, and I read every sentence of the lawsuit, a suit brought for "Separate Maintenance," and explained various portions to the kids. I answered their questions as best I could.

Did you catch something important as you read that last section? When you and I go through the storms and valleys of life, it is a frightful time not only for you and me but also for others around us—people who are close to us and love us. If we have not been in touch with our Advocate and found His words reassuring and confidence building, we are not in a position to reassure those around us and build *their* confidence.

On Monday, the papers went to Bob Kostin's office, and we set up a follow-up appointment. At that meeting, Bob returned to the two questions he had posed in the previous consultation: "Do you want to spend the rest of your life alone? Do you want to go through this process once or twice?" He explained that I *would* be going through the process *once* because I had to respond, in court, to the "separate maintenance suit" that had been filed against me. When I asked about his "twice" comment, he explained that "separate maintenance" was not a divorce, although the process was much the same—dividing assets and liabilities of the marriage—and that, unless we agreed to something else, the court would divide our assets and liabilities fifty-fifty—but we wouldn't be divorced. Furthermore, unless I either "shacked up with someone" (which thankfully he acknowledged he couldn't see me doing as a minister), I could not get married again because I would not be "divorced." A further explanation included the two basic times when people sued for "separate maintenance"—when they were an older couple who had no intention of ever remarrying or when the party filing for "separate maintenance" did not want the stigma or the blame for "filing for a divorce."

When I realized the legal and moral predicament, I asked, "Bob, as a Christian and as my lawyer, what would you advise me to do?"

He replied, "Unless you want to come back at some point in the future, should you meet a wonderful lady, fall in love, and want to get married, and file for divorce and go back through this process for a second time, I would advise you to counter-sue for divorce.

Rather matter-of-factly, I responded, "Then file the counter-suit."

Walking back to my black Chevy Tahoe in the back parking lot, I felt as though the valley was deeper and darker and the fog even more dense than ever. *Will there ever be light at the end of my tunnel? I wondered. Will this storm ever subside? Will there be an end to this valley?*

For some of us, divorce means more than losing a marriage partner of (in my case) thirty years. For those of us in vocational ministry, it can also mean the end of our ministry. In light of the fact that I was facing the possibility of a divorce, I had brought the governing board of the First Baptist Church of Davisburg into the loop several weeks earlier. But one meeting in particular stands out because during that meeting I realized that I did not have the heart to put the church through undue hardship in an effort to maintain my position as lead pastor. That evening, the good men of the board communicated that although they wanted me to continue as the senior pastor of the church, they believed that it would be necessary for my estranged wife and me to give evidence that our marriage was going to work and get everything back to normal.

After several minutes of discussion, I asked the men to quantify that "evidence" for me. One of the men spoke, enumerating three basic and reasonable actions that would provide adequate evidence; the other men remained silent but nodded their agreement. I then realized that they did not grasp the gravity of the situation. I knew in my heart at that moment that I would resign.

It seemed as though the darkness of my valley could be cut with a knife. I've never felt lonelier. In the days ahead, I even felt abandoned. *Will it ever end?* I wondered.

In spite of the advice that I had received from sixteen different minister friends from around the world not to resign, or not to resign too quickly, I knew that I did not want to damage the reputation of the church in the community. At the conclusion of a Sunday morning service shortly after that board meeting, I read my resignation announcement to a stunned and silent—except for the sniffling— congregation. The resignation would be effective in three weeks—the very week, almost to the day, that I would have served the church as pastor for nine years. I slipped out of the service during the closing prayer but lingered in the lobby to reassure those who could bring themselves to talk.

Will life ever be easier than this? Is there no end to this storm?

Three weeks later, for our final service together, I did a concert that included the songs most requested by the people. A group of musicians that included my dear friend Gary Cannon came to me and said, "Pastor, we want this concert to be extra special. Rather than doing the songs using your sound tracks, we'd like to be your live band that evening."

Reluctantly, because I'm not a well-trained musician myself (although I was a music education major in college), I agreed because of what I sensed in their eyes and voices as we chatted. All of the accompaniment music that evening was live with one exception—the closing song. I had told no one about this song—I wanted it to be my final reassurance to a heart-broken church—a congregation of people whom I loved more than any other. Like Muhammad Ali when he was on the ropes in Manila years earlier, I reached way down deep inside myself and found the confidence and assurance of the indwelling Holy Spirit to sing the classic Christian hymn, "It Is Well with My Soul."

When peace like a river attendeth my way;
When sorrows like sea billows roll;
Whatever my lot, Thou has taught me to say,
It is well, it is well with my soul.

CHORUS

It is well with my soul,
It is well, it is well with my soul.

Though Satan should buffet, though trials should come,
Let this blest assurance control—
That Christ has regarded my helpless estate
And hath shed His own blood for my soul.

But perhaps the most powerful, reassuring words, both to my own heart and to the hearts of the members and friends of First Baptist Church of Davisburg, were these:

And Lord haste the day when my faith shall be sight;
The clouds be rolled back as a scroll;
The trump shall resound, the Lord shall descend;
Even so, it is well with my soul.

It is well with my soul,
It is well, it is well with my soul.

But that night as I walked away from that congregation of believers, I felt as though much of what I loved in this world was being ripped from me—that I was being gutted, field-dressed—alive. Why? Because I was walking away from a congregation of people whom I loved deeply—a congregation that loved me deeply—and everyone was hurting. No one seemed to know what to say or do. I had not been the type of pastor who embraces the philosophy that I must go outside of the church to find friends. Through the years, I've heard several ministers state that if the pastor becomes too close to his people, they will lose respect for him as their pastor. Whenever I heard that kind of talk, it made me wonder what kind of life that man must be living that would cause people to lose respect for him as they became better acquainted with him! My desire was to so live that the more people knew about me, the more their respect for me might grow!

But on that Sunday night, none of that mattered. I was losing not only my wife of thirty years but also my church. Could it be that my church had been a part of the problem? Oh, please, don't misunderstand! The people of the church were not the problem—but perhaps the church itself had become "the other woman" in my life. Let me explain.

I've come to realized that, although I had determined in my heart and mind years earlier that my priorities in life would be, first, my personal relationship with

God; second, my relationship with my wife; third, my relationship with my children; and then my relationship with my church (which was for me also my vocation), somehow in practical terms, the church (or ministry in general) had taken top priority for years. On paper, my priorities were right and were clearly and correctly stated. In my head, my priorities were well rehearsed. However, in the reality of daily life—borne out by the clock, the calendar, and the cerebellum—my priorities had been instead the church and—well—the church— and somewhere well below was wife and children.

One of my mentors since childhood has been Dr. John Rawlings, who, for decades was the senior pastor of Landmark Baptist Temple in Cincinnati, Ohio. Dr. John (as most of us who know him well affectionately refer to him) asked me a pointed question one morning when we were both attending a national conference in Savannah, Georgia. "Son, tell me, what was *your* part in the demise of your marriage?"

Without missing a beat, I replied, "Oh, Doc, that's easy—I followed your advice!"

"What do you mean?" he retorted, bristling a bit, his back stiffening and his shoulders jerking back.

"Sixteen hours! Sixteen hours! Sixteen hours! Doc, as far back as I can remember, you 'big boys' have hammered on us younger preachers: 'If you young bucks will *work*, you can build a church!'"

As quickly as greased lightning, Dr. John exclaimed defensively, "Now, you're not going to blame the demise of your marriage on *me*!"

"No, Doc, I'm not blaming you. I'm simply answering your question by acknowledging my part in the demise of my own marriage—I chose to follow bad advice!" In spite of the sharp tone of that brief conversation, Dr. John Rawlings and I have remained good friends to this day. But there is something of great value in this exchange for every vocational minister—yea, every husband and father!

It is not enough to set our priorities on paper and in our heads; we must also make choices daily to guarantee that we live out those priorities. And, frankly, the world (cosmos) around us is hostile to those values and priorities—which, in part, explains the divorce rate in America today.

Once again, I found myself feeling as though I were on the bottom of the barrel and being smashed by the circumstances of life pressing down upon me. (It was the same feeling as before, when I had battled depression only a few years earlier.) I had only a few weeks to find a place to live and vacate the parsonage. My wife was gone; the divorce was pending. The children stayed with their mother during the week, so as not to disrupt their school schedule at Southfield Christian School in Southfield, Michigan—the only school they had ever known since kindergarten—and stayed with me on weekends. I had no job—no income—and not much will to go on with life—except for the kids. The intensity of the storm was increasing. *Will it ever end?*

But the week following my resignation, one of the businessmen of the church called and asked, "Pastor Dale, what are you going to do for income?"

Honestly, I had no real idea, so with a sign of one sinking into depression I replied, "Gary, I have no idea!"

"Then why don't you meet Angie and me for lunch today? There's something I'd like to throw at you."

Why not, I thought? *I have nothing else to do.* (At least I had nothing else that I *felt* like doing!) Later that day, I met Angie and Gary Cannon for a light lunch at the Lone Tree Bar & Grill in Highland, Michigan, not even suspecting what they might want. We had hardly taken a bite of our lunches when Gary started his brief presentation. He had a job offer for me to consider. Although the salary and benefits were a substantial drop from what I had received as a senior pastor, *something* was much better than *nothing*, so within hours I accepted the offer. Suddenly, there was another glimmer of hope shining through the terrible darkness of my storm, my valley.

After I began working as the Public Relations Director of Quantum Appraisal Company of Highland (Gary Cannon's company) in the fall of 2000, the negotiations continued toward a settlement in the divorce. The court-ordered seminars and appearances in court were no doubt designed to help the average man on the street, but they seemed to serve only as another form of humiliation. During those times and events the prevailing question on my mind was *How did I get from where I once was to this?* Indeed like the old gospel song says, "The darkness deepens."

ABIDE WITH ME

Abide with me; fast falls the eventide.

The darkness deepens; Lord with me abide.

When other helpers fail and comforts flee,

Help of the helpless, O abide with me.

Swift to its close ebbs out life's little day.

Earth's joys grow dim; its glories pass away.

Change and decay in all around I see;

O Thou who changest not, abide with me.

Hold Thou thy cross before my closing eyes;

Shine thro' the gloom and point me to the skies.

Heav'n's morning breaks, and earth's vain shadows flee.

In life, in death, O Lord, abide with me.

(Henry F. Lyte & William H. Monk)

Also in the week or so following my resignation at the church, one of the long time residents of Davisburg/ Holly and members of the church in Davisburg, David Brown, called and asked if we could have dinner one evening. That evening, as we sat at dinner in the Villager's Restaurant in Holly, a place where David's late father

Claire Brown and I had often eaten lunches together, David suddenly interrupted himself and exclaimed, "Dale, if you haven't found a place to live soon, you can live in my apartment at the house!"

Years earlier, the younger Mr. Brown had built an addition—two small bedrooms, a kitchen and dining room, a living room, and one bathroom—onto his own home on Eagle Road in Davisburg to accommodate elderly relatives. Now, having limited financial resources, facing an uncertain divorce settlement, and trying to keep my head above water emotionally, I accepted David's offer to live in his apartment, which was now vacated by the relatives, who had moved south to a warmer climate.

Meanwhile, our three minor children were facing an unfortunate decision—a decision that children should not have to face but, in the throes of life, sometimes must: With which parent would they choose to live? Their decision was gut-wrenching for me as their father; I can't imagine what it must have been like for them. Again, I never questioned them on those things—I only ensured that they knew that I loved them and that I was there for them to talk with if they so chose.

The three of them made their choices, no doubt pulled in every direction by their own thoughts and emotions. Our youngest daughter Joy (having now turned thirteen) and one of our twin boys, Joshua (fifteen years old at the time), chose to stay with me. Jordan, the other twin, and his mother moved into an apartment in a neighboring community. As if being faced with such a decision wasn't difficult enough, the two teenagers who chose to stay with me also were faced with changing schools. Perhaps it was their lack of understanding about how difficult that transition would be, but they made their selection, and the three of us moved into that small but wonderful apartment in Davisburg. Joshua and Joy each had their own bedroom but had to share dresser and closet space with their dad, which I'm sure was a delight for any teenage daughter! And for the next four years, I slept on the couch. As I drifted off to sleep many nights, I wondered, *How did I get from where I once was to here?* The valley was deep—and long—and often discouraging. *Will this storm ever blow through? Will my life ever have sunshine again?*

During the early years of the twenty-first century, although I missed my role as a pastor with my own congregation, I always had invitations to preach for other churches around the country, so I was not left feeling totally abandoned by the Christian community. I must say, however, that there isn't much demand for a divorced Baptist preacher. And yet, in the providence of God, my schedule remained comfortably full on weekends, especially during May through November of each year, when the three kids and I stayed busy performing "A Salute to America," my patriotic "road show." "Salute" was a one-hour, high-energy program incorporating live music, large-screen video projection, and message. The twins Jordan and Joshua enjoyed running all of the technical systems behind the screens (and in the dark, I might add), while Joy ran the lighting system during the show and manned the product table before and after the performances. It isn't uncommon to hear the kids tell stories about those road trips even to this day, especially about various events that transpired aboard the tour bus, which had been converted into a luxury motor coach.

Then came the spring—but with the spring 2001 also came April 25 and that final court appearance before the Honorable Judge Joan E. Young in the Circuit Court of Oakland County, Michigan. There was no need for breakfast—I was not in the frame of mind to eat. After getting the children off to school, I dressed in absolute silence in the apartment and made my way down Dixie Highway toward Pontiac, and then to the locally famous (or infamous) 1200 Telegraph Road, home for the Oakland County government complex, including the Circuit Court.

Only three or four people were in the courtroom when I arrived—a couple of court officers moving in and out shuffling papers of that morning's session and a couple of other people in the seating gallery. Not seeing Bob Kostin, my attorney, I sat on a pew near the main entry to the courtroom. Although the pew resembled those in many church auditoriums that had been "home" to me for more than thirty years, my gut told me that this environment was different—and the sick feeling in my stomach grew. Even when the familiar figure of my attorney popped through the door and he greeted me exuberantly, my thought was *What are* you *so happy about while* my *life is falling apart?* (In retrospect, I understand that he was smiling because he was making $6,000 while I was losing more than half of everything I owned!) But I mustered a faint smile and returned his greeting.

After laying out his paperwork on the defendant's table and telling me that he and I would be seated there, he walked across the courtroom to the plaintiff's table and exchanged words with Scott Sitner, the lawyer retained by my soon-to-be former wife. When the two attorneys were satisfied that all was in order to proceed, Bob returned to the defendant's table and motioned for me to join him there. We were seated until we heard the bailiff announce in a rather matter-of-fact manner, "All rise! Court is now in session, the honorable Judge Joan E. Young presiding!"

My blood ran cold! Time now seemed to slow to a crawl. I barely heard the instructions, "Be seated, please!"

I had barely touched the chair when the attorneys, my wife, and I were asked to stand again as our suit and docket numbers were called. Interspersed with the continuing thoughts of *How did I get from where I once was to here?* were frightful thoughts of what was going to happen, what it all meant, and what would happen to the children. Perhaps most haunting of all was when Judge Young turned and looked deeply into my eyes for what seemed like an eternity. It was as though she were trying to extract from me, through my eye contact with her, everything about me. And from her eyes, I gathered that she understood that my world as a minister was being turned upside down, if not totally destroyed.

Within a matter of minutes, the gavel rapped the desk, and by the very words of a stranger in a black robe, a marriage of thirty years was dissolved. What God had joined together, indeed man (or, in that courtroom, anyway, woman) *had* put asunder. With a handshake, congratulation, and an offer to assist if anything else was needed in the future, a very gracious Bob Kostin said goodbye. As I walked out into the fresh spring sunshine, I did not have the feeling of great freedom but rather the feeling that something was missing. *How can this be? How can someone, even a duly sworn judge – who knows absolutely nothing about my family, my marriage, or me – simply eradicate a thirty-year marriage? It's over – just like that?* I didn't know what to do next. What *does* one do when he doesn't know what to do? You do what you *know* to do. So I went back to my office at Quantum Appraisal Services, where I was greeted with surprise.

I can still hear Angie Cannon ask in bewilderment, "Why are you here?" Several other appraisers and support staff members sat at their desks equally bewildered but saying nothing. I simply mumbled, "I didn't know where else to go, but since it's a work day, I assumed that I should get back to work as soon as possible." Kind-hearted clan that they were, each coworker assured me that it would be okay if I took the rest of the day off, so I did.

But let me come back to this business of "What God hath joined together, let not man put asunder" for a moment. Believe me, I now understand something that, before my own divorce, I never understood. Heck, I don't even claim to understand it *completely* now—but I have learned a few things from that horrible experience. It would be sinful for me to waste my pain by failing to help others to avoid the same or similar circumstances if at all possible. So let me try "digging a well in the valley" right here.

A divorce is not always—perhaps seldom is—a clean surgical separation of two people who have become one. When two young people (in our case, I was twenty and my former wife was nineteen when we were married on Saturday, August 1, 1970, in Allen Park, Michigan) make the commitment to each other before an officiate (whether minister, judge, magistrate, priest, rabbi, or captain of a ship), and before witnesses, they have little, if any, clue what that will mean in the years to come. But on the basis of their romantic, emotional, and intellectual commitment, they pledge to ride out whatever storms may overtake them in life. And while most of us realize that storms are indeed a part of life and that no one gets from the cradle to the grave without enduring some storms, it seems never to move from the theoretical form—until the storm actually blows into our lives. Sometimes, some of us are so busy with whatever it is that has worked its way to the top of our priorities in real daily life that we don't even notice the clouds gathering on the horizon of our lives. At other times, we erroneously assume that somehow the problems, the symptoms, and the mistakes of life will simply go away or rectify themselves. That simply is not true.

Others view a divorce as a clean, surgical separation that will be little more than a proverbial bump in the road, and life will go on, business as usual. However, that is seldom the case either. Usually, trust has been violated. Dreams have been shattered. Only the most calloused of humanity would move on unaffected and unscathed by a divorce. Rather than divorce being the clean cut of a legal scalpel by the skilled and trained hand of a surgeon (attorney or judge), it is a ripping apart of what God has joined together, a "tearing apart" of what had become *one*. Only in the aftermath of a divorce, whether bitter or civil, does one begin to understand the biblical admonition that Jesus Christ Himself quotes in the gospels of Matthew and Mark:

(Matt 19:6 KJV) Wherefore they are no more twain, but one flesh. What therefore God hath joined together, let not man put asunder.

(Mark 10:9 KJV) What therefore God hath joined together, let not man put asunder.

Some damage is obvious; some isn't.

One spouse, perhaps even both spouses, will have to move out of the house where the family has lived. Potentially, that necessity might create financial hardship for the spouse who remains. It might also create a hardship for the spouse who is moving out. Certainly, emotional struggles can result from the loss of the home and furniture and even in the division of simple household items, such as kitchen items, family pictures and heirlooms, and even "the junk" that has collected through the years, stored away in boxes in the attic or basement and out of sight for decades. Division of assets of all kinds means downsizing for both partners and represents a change that can often be traumatic. It might mean driving smaller, less expensive vehicles. Scaling back might mean living for a time in an apartment rather than in a luxurious house in one of the better neighborhoods. It certainly means making fewer dollars go farther for many divorcees when it comes to shopping at the grocery store, dining out, or selecting entertainment and recreation. That "damage" can be somewhat obvious to close friends and family who are looking in on the situation.

However, some damage is unseen—tucked away in the privacy of the individual heart. It might be the sting of betrayal, whether the life-partner simply and slowly drifted away emotionally or there was blatant infidelity—or both. The very sense of rejection by a spouse is a horrific unseen source of damage. And to any reader who has experienced such rejection and betrayal, let me remind you that, first, I understand what that feels

like, and, second, you can *grow* through even that difficult experience. But you must *choose* for yourself to do
so. Stop looking in the rearview mirror of your life at
yesterday. Stop blaming your former spouse and love of
your life. Deliberately acknowledge what has happened,
mentally do an about face, and focus on tomorrow.

What do you want your tomorrow to look like? The
apostle Paul gave wise advice when he penned these
words: "Brethren, I do not count myself to have appre-
hended; but one thing I do, forgetting those things which
are behind and reaching forward to those things which
are ahead" (Phil. 3:13 New King James Version) That
means you might have to remind yourself many times
that the ideal for which you had hoped is gone, and no
matter how badly you still wish that it had worked out, it
didn't. So now what should you do? Forget those things
which are behind.

Does that mean that we can't remember the good
times? No. Does that mean that we will always forget
everything of the past? No. However, it does mean that
we must consciously determine in our minds that whenever we sense that our thought processes related to the
past are pulling us down, no matter when it happens or

how often it happens, we must at that moment re-focus toward the future. In the early stages of separation and divorce, this can be especially difficult, in part because the emotional pain is so fresh. That is when we most often must remind ourselves to face the future.

Please understand, too, that to face the future and forget the past does not mean that we pretend that the past never happened. It *did* happen—whatever it was— the good, the bad, the ugly. So don't pretend that it did not happen. The question is not whether it did or did not happen but what we will choose to do with our life today? Someone wisely proclaimed that "today is the first day of the rest of your life." Get a realistic picture firmly in your mind of what you want the rest of your life to look like, and then outline the goals, objectives, and steps that you must take to arrive at that picture. Once you have established those new goals, take the daily actions and steps necessary to move you toward the new picture that you painted in your mind's eye.

Will this process be an easy one? No, it will not always be easy. However, if your tomorrow is to be better than your yesterday, it is your responsibility to take the actions today that will move you to that better tomorrow.

Life is not about yesterday, even though we can learn from and be motivated by understanding our yester-days. We have already lived our yesterdays. We cannot live our tomorrows until they arrive, which means that the only reasonable and responsible action we can take is to live today!

Following my own advice is what helped me to survive and then to thrive. I realized that if I refused to yield to the discouragements and defeats of the valleys of life, I would eventually come out of the valley and find sunshine on the other side of the storms. But that can take far longer than any of us want it to while its happening! For example, during the time that I was employed by the real estate appraisal firm, my friend encouraged me to continue my education, complete the required course work, and secure my Limited Real Estate Appraiser's license in Michigan—which I did. However, as I began my work, I learned that, being the low man on the totem pole of the company, my work was almost always out of town—*far out* of town—as on the other side of the state of Michigan. Although I could do the work, and although my friend and owner of the company had been very generous with me, I began to struggle with two aspects of my work. First, because I was traveling to Battle Creek, Kalamazoo, Grand Rapids, Muskegon, and a dozen little townships around western Michigan, I was leaving home by 6:00 a.m., and often not returning until early evening. That's a problem for a single dad with two teenage children in school. It meant that they were on their own most mornings to get up, prepare their own breakfast, dress, and get out the door and to school on-time. And don't forget—*they* were struggling, too!

In fact, it wasn't until well after both Joshua and Joy had graduated from high school that Joshua shared with me some of the details of their struggles. Remember, they had left the only school they had known since kindergarten and enrolled in a new one, Joshua entering tenth grade and Joy entering seventh grade. During the first several months of the school year, I drove them to school early each morning, dropping them off well before other students began to arrive so that I could get to work on time at Quantum Appraisal. Thankfully, a young woman named Karen Rosell from my former church in Davisburg was kind enough to transport them from school to home again each afternoon. Later, when Joshua could drive, he drove them. As they pulled into the drop-off zone at the middle school, Joy often pleaded with Joshua to wait with her until the last minute, which he would do. He tried to console her as she cried—hating the transition and dreading another day of school away from the friends with whom she had grown up in earlier years.

Perhaps most gut-wrenching of all for me as their father was when Joshua told me this story. Then he revealed that although he had tried always to be strong for Joy, after dropping her off at the middle school, he often pulled across the street into the student parking lot at Fenton High School, where he sat and wept, too. When he could "get it together," he headed into the high school, often tardy for his own class. I'll never truly know the pain those children went through, but I know that we made it—together.

One of the ways the three of us encouraged ourselves in those days was reading together the small book *Who Moved My Cheese?* That book made a huge impact on each of us, including Joshua's twin brother Jordan. Although the children were teenagers at the time, I sat down with them in the living room of our tiny apartment, usually on weekends, and we read a portion of the book together and discussed how we could apply the principles to our situation. Although I sometimes doubted the value of doing that with three teenagers, I learned recently that it had paid off when Jordan text-messaged me years later asking if he could borrow that book. He remembered the benefit it had been to him, and when he was going through a valley experience of his own as a graduate student at New York University, he thought it would be beneficial for him to re-read the book on his own!

We also encouraged one another in another way. Joshua had discovered a few boxes of sermons on cassette tapes that I had saved for years. He commandeered them to listen to at night, in his spare time, or when he was driving in his 1992 GMC Jimmy. One of those sermons that he came across had been preached by the late Dr. Jack Hudson, from Charlotte, North Carolina. The sermon was titled "It's Friday Now, But Sunday's Coming." The message had been recorded at the Temple Baptist Church of Powell, Tennessee, during their annual Dogwood Bible Conference. Although the early moments of the message dealt primarily with the Crucifixion on Good Friday, it was laced with the great hope that a Resurrection Sunday was just around the bend! The kids listened to that sermon on their drive to school most mornings for a long time—reminding themselves that although life was tough at the moment, better days were just ahead.

Here's the point of my sharing those details from my children's lives: find a way to encourage yourself while you are going through the valley—a book, a CD, an old cassette tape, a quiet place to reflect. Perhaps in your life right now, it's Crucifixion Friday. Don't forget that although it's Friday now, Sunday's coming. A resurrection of life is just ahead of you, my friend. Believe that. Look for that. And although it might seem a long time in coming, wait for it!

Joshua shared with me one day in the fall of 2008 a few of his random thoughts and memories. Included among them is his testimony to the power of music to lift the suffering human heart.

All of us were in uncharted territory. Emotional stress would have been an understatement.

(I remember a) single father entering the secular job market for the first time, working to pay off debt and provide for his 15 year-old-boy and 13-year-old girl.

(We were t)wo private/Christian school kids entering the seemingly unwelcoming social context of the public school system halfway through the semester, leaving behind life-long friends and all things familiar. (We were thrust into a) new church, new school, new life ... none of which had come by our choice. This was not a welcoming or exciting adventure.

We were used to a large house, where we each had our own rooms, enjoyed a huge yard and had plenty of personal space and comfort. Being young teenagers, doing without material comforts of the house we grew up in is one of the things I remember first. The tiny apartment the three of us had to share only had two bedrooms. For nearly four years, my sister and I watched our Dad sleep on a couch, in order to give his children the privacy and comfort of their own bedrooms. That wasn't the only thing he sacrificed for us. Without having full knowledge of the amount of cash Dad had at any given time, we knew that money was tight to say the least. Joy and I were both too young to get a job, so for the first few months, on a weekly basis, we would watch him open his wallet and take out all the money he had at the time (usually no more than 8 or 12 dollars) and give it to us as our lunch money for the week.

But in the midst of those dark days, God was able to display his provision and comfort in remarkable ways. In fact, it was in those hard times that he brought about some of the most encouraging moments ... moments where the presence of the Holy Spirit was more real than I could have ever imagined, and our love for the Lord and each other was strengthened in a way that could never be accomplished in a time of peace and prosperity.

Those moments often came early in the morning while Dad was driving Joy and me to school. He had to drop us off much earlier than the other kids, because he had to begin an hour-long commute to work from our school. Sometimes we would listen to sermons, desperately searching for a Word from God to get us through. Perhaps even more memorable to me were the days we would sing. It's amazing how God can move

through music. After coming through the loneliness and depression of those days, and remem-
bering so clearly the way God used music to bring
unity, comfort and encouragement to our family,
it's no wonder that some of the greatest songs of
the faith were written by men and women going
through the darkest valleys of their lives. An old
Ray Boltz song stands out in my mind, and the
morning that the three of us held hands in the
car and sang through tears and whimpers, " ...
no matter what tomorrow brings or what it has
in store, I know, I will praise the Lord!"

But let me get back to the long days of traveling
throughout Michigan as a real estate appraiser.

After being gone many days from early morning
until early evening, I came home to spend a few hours
typing reports but not spending very much quality
time with Joshua and Joy. I was of little benefit to them
with their homework because I was consumed with
my own homework—typing reports each night from
the appraisals that I had conducted during the day! I
struggled with how to keep going, struggled to become

proficient at a new career, and struggled emotionally, I often felt that the kids were a greater support to me than I was to them, which only increased my personal struggle with unnecessary guilt. I also struggled with who I was. *How did I get from where I once was to where I now found myself—sitting in the living room, which also served as my bedroom and my office, typing appraisals?* I asked myself. *Will there ever be an end to this valley?*

Early one morning, my pastor and friend Terry Rudd and I were meeting for breakfast. It was not uncommon for Terry to bring with him something to pass along to me—something that he thought might be an encouragement. On that particular morning, he tossed a workbook onto the table as he sat down across from me.

"I thought you might want to look through that workbook and see if that's something that would interest you," he said. Not waiting for a response, he continued, "We [meaning First Baptist Church of Pontiac] have a new quarter beginning in a couple of weeks for our singles ministry on Wednesday evenings. This quarter they'll be using this workbook." After Terry rushed off to another appointment after breakfast, I sat for a few minutes, sipping my coffee and thumbing through the book.

Once again, I found myself thinking, *How did I get from where I once was to where I am now — thumbing through a Divorce Care® workbook and contemplating attending a self-help group for divorcees?* But I soon shook myself "awake" to the reality that I *am* divorced. I'm not the first, and I don't have a clue what steps to take next. I also thought that if my friend thought I should do this, then I would do it. I enrolled in the course.

I'll never forget that first night. I was one of about twenty participants who sat in a classroom at the church. After we all introduced ourselves and the leaders briefly explained the evening's events, we watched a thirty-minute video—the first in the series from Divorce Care®. We then took a ten-minute break before dividing into two small groups for discussion. A gentleman who has since become one of my dearest friends, Jim Coram, was leading my particular small group. He began by explaining how the group would function. Whatever was shared by anyone in the group stayed in the group, and everyone was encouraged to share his or her "story" and struggles. But first, Jim stated, he wanted each of us to rate our week, on a scale from one to ten, with one being the worst week of our lives and ten being the best.

As though it had just this second happened, I remember Jim saying, "And I always start to my left."

I was seated immediately to Jim Coram's left, so I was to begin the process of giving my name, telling my story, and rating my week. Although I've never attended a meeting of Alcoholics Anonymous, I felt inside as though I should say, "Hi. My name is Dale, and I'm an alcoholic!" It all felt so strange, and deep inside was the haunting question, screaming from the innermost part of my being, *How did I get from where I was to here?* Somehow, I mumbled and stumbled my way through that initial, informal presentation, no doubt setting a poor example for others to either follow or improve upon.

Yet, through all of those awkward, embarrassing, and even humiliating moments, God was working through other people and in my life. Later, I would discover that He was actually using my own weaknesses to offer encouragement and hope to others around me—which is a part of the strength of small groups like those who met for Divorce Care®, Divorce Recovery, and Living Single Again that met on Wednesday nights at my church.

Sometimes, I felt as though my long-time friend Terry Rudd had "handed me off" to his associate

Dennis Henderson, who lead the singles ministries of the church, and yet, even if that had been the case, it was a good thing. Dennis had once been the lead pastor of a growing church in Ohio. Through circumstances very similar to my own, Dennis ended up back home in Michigan where he had grown up. He was now serving on the pastoral staff of First Baptist Church of Pontiac. He certainly understood—experientially—what I was going through. Terry recognized that fact as well and had wisely brought Dennis into my life to come alongside me as a human "paraclete," or comforter, and one for whom I will be eternally grateful.

My cell phone rang one afternoon. A Christian businessman from our church, First Baptist Church of Pontiac—the oldest Baptist church in Michigan—asked if we could set a time to have lunch one day that week. He had something he wanted to run by me. In a few days, Dave Henderson, (brother to Dennis Henderson, who God was using greatly to undergird and encourage me), and I sat down together in an area restaurant for lunch. Dave began to share the story of his "dot.com" company, which was named See Progress, Inc. It is a high-end technology company related to the automotive and insurance industries, and its growth had been remarkable, especially that of its primary focus division, AutoWatch®. The company was interested in beginning a new division called CampWatch®, and the management of See Progress, Inc., was interested in bringing me on-board to help create that new division. It would target youth camps around the country and assist them in their Internet operations. The salary, though modest, was enough on which to live and care for my children; health insurance was also a benefit, as were several expense-related items. Best of all, the company was headquartered in Farmington Hills, Michigan, which was less than a thirty-minute drive from home! I accepted the offer and began work a few weeks later.

Although we enjoyed modest success getting that fledgling division off the ground, after one year CampWatch® was still not self-supporting. Upon review by the parent company's management team, they determined that continuing for a second year, using borrowed funds for operations, was not feasible. My dear friend Dave Henderson had the difficult assignment of breaking the news to me. I can only hope that how I received that news made his task a wee bit easier. Nonetheless, in a few weeks, I would again be unemployed. That's sort of like—well—another mile or so in the valley! *Will there ever be an end to the valley?* I found myself wondering yet again. *Will I ever be able truly to get back on my feet?*

But then one day the phone rang. Remember Reverend Terry Rudd? He's not only my friend but also he was also my pastor during my time in the valley of my life, and he wanted to have breakfast with me the next day! (After a while, you gotta love meal time when the chips are down, because it seems like something good always comes from meal time when the chips are down!) So the following morning, Terry and I had breakfast together at Ripples, a local institution that's been around since—well—I think Noah's first meal off the boat was at Ripples!

Terry was following up with me about an e-mail that I had written him earlier about a staff position at First Baptist Church of Pontiac, located in White Lake, not far from Ripples restaurant. We discussed some of the details of that "utility" position on the support staff at the church. The primary function would be to coordinate all of the custodial and maintenance work. That would be quite a step down from where I had been in the past as the senior pastor of a growing church, but it *would* move me in the direction that I wanted to go and a workload that I understood very well from three decades of experience. By the time I completed my work with See Progress, Inc., and CampWatch®, the process at the church was complete for me to join the staff there. The good hand of God was everywhere I turned at First Baptist Church. I was privileged to pastor and teach a wonderful young married class about whom I cannot say enough good. I told them several times (and still believe this is true) that they were a greater help to me than I ever could have been to them.

Another ministry of vital importance to our church, our community, and me personally was Singles, Inc., which included a vibrant ministry to those who had gone through or were going through a divorce. Under the leadership of Dr. Dennis Henderson, many of us began to find solutions to many of the circumstances that life handed us and strength for the journey of life again as we interacted with each other week after week. It provided an excellent opportunity for total strangers to become dear friends, as many of us did. Most of us, upon entering our introductory quarter—whether that was Divorce Care®, Divorce Recovery, or Living Single Again—did not even want to be there and were in shock that we were going through or had been through a divorce, complete with our feelings that no one in the world understood what we were experiencing. However, it usually took only a few weeks of interacting through the video or lecture segments, the small group discussions, and a less formal time of chatting over refreshments before new participants were making new friends and others were deepening friendships already begun.

In fact, one of the greatest things to come from those days on the staff of First Baptist Church, particularly from my involvement leading a small group in the divorce recovery ministry, was a friendship with a wonderful woman named Debbie Johns, who on Saturday, November 1, 2008, would become Mrs. Debbie Peterson! Great things *can* happen, even in the valleys of our lives. In fact, that's one of the things that my youngest son Joshua noted earlier, wasn't it? But in the midst of the storms and the valleys, when fear would overtake us, we must deliberately remind ourselves that "there's still One who cares for you, Jesus never fails!" We discover renewed courage, faith, hope, and strength as we divert our attention from the fearful storm and refocus on "the Master of ocean and earth and sky."

[Debbie and Dale Peterson at Niagara Falls]

Winding our way through the valley experiences in life always seems to take longer than we would prefer, but usually, in retrospect, we discover that the time flew by, although it seemed to creep at a snail's pace while we were in the valley. Perhaps one of the great lessons of life we learn from the valley is patience. God never works on *our* time table; rather, we are to work on *His*, allowing

Him to do all that He chooses as He chooses. Although it has not always been with seasoned patience—I was more like the unbroken horse fighting against the strange bit and bridle that a skilled ranch hand uses—I *am* learning. The valleys of life have been my classrooms, and the storms have been my professors.

Can I encourage you to look beyond the disappointments, fears, frustrations, and pain of your immediate circumstances? You must not permit the emotion of the immediate to control your future. Whenever we find ourselves in some storm or valley along the road of life, we are tempted to make decisions while we are emotionally supercharged or super discouraged. That is always dangerous because emotion tends to override solid, rational thinking. We risk being paralyzed by our fears, being drawn into unhealthy relationships, or venturing irrationally into activities that might offer a momentary relief from our pain or distraction from otherwise solid steps forward as we deal with our valley experience.

Another song that offered me great council comes to my mind—*Joy Comes in the Morning*, written by Bill Gaither years ago.

If you've knelt beside the rubble

Of an aching broken heart

When the things you gave your life to

Fell apart

You're not the first to be acquainted

With sorrow grief or pain

But the master promised sunshine

After rain

CHORUS

Hold on my child

Joy comes in the morning

Weeping only lasts for the night

Hold on my child

Joy comes in the morning

The darkest hour means dawn

Is just in sight

To invest your seed of trust in God

In mountains you can't move

You have risked your life on things

You cannot prove

But to give the things you cannot keep

For what you cannot lose

Is the way to find the joy
God has for you

Hold on my child
Joy comes in the morning
Weeping only lasts for the night
Hold on my child
Joy comes in the morning
The darkest hour means dawn
Is just in sight

I can suggest that course of action with confidence and experience. I can, I will, and I do! Sometimes I really felt like throwing in the towel. That was temptation. To be tempted to quit is not wrong, but to *act* on that temptation to give up when life became difficult *would* have been wrong. Dr. Bob Jones, Sr., evangelist and founder of the South Carolina university that bears his name, was known especially for his "chapel sayings." One of them was, "Do right! If the stars fall, do right!" That would apply to people who are going through tough times as well although it might not always be the easiest thing to do. But, given enough time, it will always lead to an honorable conclusion.

A few years ago, after the divorce and in preparation for a Thanksgiving Day dinner, I had asked my children to give some serious thought to things for which each of them were thankful. That afternoon as we gathered around the table, the children took turns sharing their thoughts. Suddenly, Joshua said, "Dad, you haven't shared anything yet!"

"I'm waiting on each of you to finish because I only have one thing that I want to share today," I replied.

Soon the children had exhausted their lists, and each turned to look in my direction, as if to say, "Okay, Dad, it's your turn!"

Here is what I shared with them that Thanksgiving Day, and I think it's worthy of your consideration. "I am thankful that life goes on (although at times I wished that it wouldn't) because I have discovered that I always come to a time when I'm glad that life *did* go on!"

Does that make sense to you? You see, in spite of the fact that on several days in my past I was so discouraged that I was tempted just to quit, I didn't. Sometimes it was because I had responsibilities with the children. At other times it was because I knew that the right thing to do was to keep going. Inevitably, for whatever reason at the moment, I kept going until the valley *du' jour* was in the rearview mirror of my life.

I continue an itinerate ministry, speaking throughout the United States and in a few foreign countries each year. I have a special focus on developing youth leaders in Great Britain through the mechanism of Strategic Youth Leadership Summits, a division of Gospel Alive, Inc., a Michigan-based 501(c)3 organization I founded in 1984. I see God's faithfulness not only in a fresh direction for ministry but also in marriage. In November 2008, I was married to Debbie Johns, the wonderful lady whom I met in 2003 through the divorce care ministry of my church and through which I was "digging a well" by translating my pain into other people's gain as they went through the valley of divorce.

Are you going through some valley, perhaps a separation or divorce? Are you frustrated by your circumstances? Are you fearful about what your future might hold? Are you confused about what step to take next?

My friend, although you might not understand what has happened or what to do next, God has not overlooked you, your circumstances, or your feelings. Will you trust Him even when His purpose for your life seems obscure? If you will, it can bring a new level of peace to your life—that peace that passes all understanding of which the apostle Paul wrote in Philippians 4:7. And in your new determination to trust Jesus Christ, why not also determine to

Leave a well in the valley, the dark and lonesome valley;
Others have to cross this valley, too:
What a blessing when they find the well of joy
you've left behind;
So, leave a well in the valley you go through.

Scriptures on Which to Meditate

(Psalm 139:17–18 New Living Translation)

How precious are your thoughts about me, O God! They are innumerable! I can't even count them; they outnumber the grains of sand! And when I wake up in the morning, you are still with me!

(Romans 15:4 New Living Translation)

Such things were written in the Scriptures long ago to teach us. They give us hope and encouragement as we wait patiently for God's promises.

(Proverbs 4:20–27 New Living Translation)

Pay attention, my child, to what I say. Listen carefully. Don't lose sight of my words. Let them penetrate deep within your heart, for they bring life and radiant health to anyone who discovers their meaning. Above all else, guard your heart, for it affects everything you do.

Avoid all perverse talk; stay far from corrupt speech. Look straight ahead, and fix your eyes on what lies before you. Mark out a straight path for your feet; then stick to the path and stay safe. Don't get sidetracked; keep your feet from following evil.

9

When Friends Disappoint You

At the outset, the reader must understand several things concerning my heart, mind, and soul.

First, although each incident that follows has some negative repercussions, I do not name names in negative circumstances. Although *Leave A Well in the* Valley is written autobiographically, use of personal experiences similar to those of other people throughout the world does not make it a "tell all" book designed to make the author look good at the expense of someone else's character.

Second, I hold absolutely no malice in my heart toward any of the individuals or groups included in this chapter. Although I have been left hurting at times, I have continually determined to release those who hurt me, love them still, and move on with life and ministry, believing that what happens *to* me is much less important than what happens *in* me. God can and will use every negative circumstance of our lives if we will allow him to do so.

Third, to the best of my knowledge, I have a clean, clear relationship with each person referred to anywhere in these pages, at least from my perspective.

Now, let's wade into this risky territory of relationships and determine to look past the hurt (not ignore it) and consider the potential growth that is available to us as we travel the road of life.

Defrauded by a trusted employer

I had taken the job offer and relocated my family some six hundred miles from our home in East Tennessee on the promise of a certain salary-and-benefit package, including major medical and hospitalization insurance, a company-owned and -maintained vehicle, paid vacations, and the promise of advancement. No longer would I be risking "losing my shirt" in my own start-up construction company but rather enjoying the security of a solid job and income.

The owner of the construction company for whom I was working often met with me early in the morning, especially on Mondays, at area restaurants to enjoy breakfast and coffee while discussing the work projects and schedules for the week. (Those Daly Restaurant sweet rolls were some of the best I had ever eaten!) Although I don't remember having a job "title," it could be considered a construction manager position or construction superintendent job. I coordinated several buildings that were under construction—a couple of residential homes, a few additions to houses, and repairs to others. But the job involved more than supervision; it included doing a lot of the physical work as well. At times, that included manual labor, including tasks that I did not do in my own little company in Tennessee but that I was now having to do during the winter and spring in Michigan. In spite of those little annoyances, I was hopeful of the future and growing with the company.

In late spring or early summer, the pediatricians and ear, nose, and throat specialists recommended that our toddler-aged daughter Charity, who had been susceptible to numerous ear infections, have surgery to implant "tubes" in her ears. That was a relatively new procedure in the early 1970s and was quite scary to my wife and me as young parents, not even in our mid-twenties, but we agreed to follow the doctors' advice and scheduled the surgery. A few days before the surgery, it dawned on me that I had not received an insurance card, and asked the owner of the construction company about it.

My boss's response flabbergasted me. It was a rather disappointed but as-matter-of-fact, "Oh, I forgot to tell you that I wasn't able to work that [insurance] out."

In disbelief, I asked, "So you're telling me that when my wife and I take our daughter to St. Joseph Mercy Hospital in Pontiac next week for surgery, I have no insurance?"

"I really feel badly about that," he continued, "but I just haven't been able to find an insurance policy that we could afford."

Dumbfounded, and not quite knowing what else to say or do, I walked away, afraid and wondering what I was going to do. How could I go home and explain to my young wife that we were facing the unknown cost of the surgery without medical insurance? That was virgin territory for us as a young couple, and we were afraid. But our daughter needed the surgery.

Thankfully, the financial department of the hospital understood our dilemma and helped us work out a viable solution that would service all parties involved. They sold our financial obligation to a small finance company and we made monthly payments that we could afford until the balance was paid in full. My relationship with strangers (i.e., St. Joseph Mercy Hospital) was intact. My relationship with the surgeon was intact because his bill was being handled through the billing department of the hospital.

However, my relationship with my employer was now strained, at least for me. We had agreed to a financial arrangement and, although I had done the work, I was not being paid in full as agreed and was now being forced to pay "a penalty"—hundreds of dollars—out of pocket because my employer did not honor his part of the agreement to provide health insurance. My heart ached. I felt betrayed. I was angry. But what should I do? How should I proceed? Should I act as if nothing had happened and everything was just fine?

As I struggled with what to do long term, I continued to maintain my daily workload as though nothing was wrong—at least that's what (hopefully) it was on the outside. On the inside, however, I was struggling. I had been "cheated" out of my insurance by a trusted employer and family friend and was having to take money from an already too-tight family budget to pay for the surgery.

One afternoon as I drove my company van east along Interstate 94 from a job site in Romulus or Belleville to our home in Taylor, I was pouring my heart out to God in prayer. I remember telling God that I felt like a failure, that I had put money and personal security ahead of doing His will with my life, and that I could think of only one thing that I could do to correct the situation—go back to where I last remembered being "in" His will—which would mean moving back to East Tennessee and start all over.

Perhaps that seems quite naïve to an onlooker, but in retrospect I realize that there was something rather innocent and pure about what was happening in my heart and mind. I wanted to do with my life whatever God wanted me to do, and I assumed that those negative circumstances were either God's punishment or His means of growing and directing my steps.

Years earlier, as a child sitting at the supper table in our modest farm house in Tennessee, I had sat with my family and memorized such Bible verses as Psalm 37:23: "The steps of a good man are ordered by the LORD: and he delighteth in his way" (KJV). And as naïve as it might seem to some people, I truly believed those words and wanted to live them out in my daily life. Shouldn't that be the result of our believing the Bible—that believing produces obedience from a heart that wants to follow God?

Sometimes we tend to treat life as though today's negative circumstance is the last chapter in our lives. To be sure, a day will come when that is true, but that doesn't mean that it's the end of the story or that "the game" is over. Be assured that God is keeping the score. Trust Him. Let go of hurts and hangups, and leave them in God's hands. You might be thinking, *But, Dale, do you really want me to believe that it's that easy?* Well, it is that *simple*, but that does not necessarily make it *easy* at the time. Letting go and leaving a problem with God is a step of faith. Can you trust God to do for you what is right when others have done what is wrong? That is often the core issue.

Meanwhile, let's go back to the after-work ride home in the company van. It was only a few miles and minutes from the time I prayed my prayer of surrender along I-94 near Detroit's Metropolitan Airport until I arrived home to a ringing telephone. (This was long before cellular telephones.) As though it happened only moments ago, I recall racing through the front door of our little bungalow at 6366 Beech-Daly Road in Taylor, Michigan, grabbing the slim line wall phone by the kitchen door to discover God's solution to my family's dilemma. Three weeks later, I was not moving backward to Tennessee but forward to my first full-time ministry position.

Sometimes we hear people say things such things as "God just wants to see if you are willing to—(you fill in the blank)." I have no doubt that God already knows our hearts, but He is often waiting on us to grow to the intersection of our past and our future. It is at that intersection where God brings the right people and provisions together at the right place and the right moment in time.

Asked to do wrong by a trusted colleague

One might expect that the business world might have an abundance of persons who might use unscrupulous ethics to make the sale, get the promotion, or avoid an organizational or personal calamity. In fact, local and national news programs routinely contain leading stories of such graft and corruption. For example, the governor of Illinois was recently impeached, a internationally known billionaire was recently sentenced to prison for more years than he can possibly live, and the extravagance of multiple CEO's is being deplored and resented by millions of American taxpayers whose children and grandchildren will be paying off trillions of dollars of national debt due in part to bailouts of large American corporations by the federal government.

However "normal" those breeches in proper ethics might be in the business world today, I never cease to be amazed when they periodically (and increasingly) are discovered among ministers. If there is a people group in the world that should consistently live up to proper ethics, one would expect that the ministry world would be at the front of the line. However, a church is merely a microcosm of the community in which it exists, and it is possible to find any form of sin *in* the church that one might find *outside* the church. Sometimes the indiscretions are subtle; at other times the violations are flagrant.

In the 1980s, the fall of televangelist Jim Bakker was splashed across newspapers, magazines, and television screens for months. That scandal was soon followed by similar immoral actions by another Southern televangelist, Jimmy Swaggart, and local, national, and international ministries all felt the fallout almost immediately. The "big sins" certainly command a lot of attention, but what about the "little things"? After all, doesn't the Bible remind us that it is the little foxes that spoil the vines? Is it possible that people, churches, and other ministries can be negatively affected by sins that might be categorized as "little white lies"? I think so.

Some years ago, a colleague put me between the proverbial rock and a hard place. The ministry in which we were both very active was struggling with cash flow. We were both successful in selling our annual budgets and gaining initial approvals for almost everything we sought. However, cash flow sometimes was a different story, and it was becoming increasingly worse.

One day, my friend and colleague (whom I will call "John") and I were discussing some of our individual and mutual projects, when I was asked to approach the comptroller and "sell" one of John's projects—but using information that was false. At the time of the conversation, I did not recoil and refuse to do as had been requested of me. I was afraid to call it the way I saw it. Rather, I walked away struggling with what to do. I hated being put in that position, but I also hated to bluntly refuse my friend John.

What made the dilemma worse was the fact that the comptroller had been my best friend for years (and still is to this day). Regrettably, I did not handle the entire scenario in the best possible manner. Rather than resolving the impropriety with my friend John, I chose to confide in my best friend, the comptroller, who could give thumbs up or thumbs down to the financial request on the basis of cash flow alone. If memory serves me correctly, the project did receive the requested funding but under increased scrutiny—and under a shadow that I had cast across the character of my friend John.

Perhaps you're asking, *What should Dale have done differently?* or *What was wrong with the way you handled the situation?*

First, I was afraid of speaking the truth humbly and lovingly to my friend John at the time he confronted me with a less-than-ethical request. Quite often in life, the things that we should not fear, we do, and the things of which we should be afraid, we aren't. When we fear doing what is right, especially with friends, we can know that we aren't handling the problem correctly.

The scriptures teach us that "God hath not given us the spirit of fear; but of power, and of love, and of a sound mind" (2 Timothy 1:7). When it comes to doing the right thing in the right way, we should not fear, but rather face our circumstances with faith. Faith and fear are on opposite ends of the spectrum. In the Old Testament, Jehovah admonished Israel's newly appointed leader, Joshua, to be strong and courageous as he faced the tasks thrust upon him. Courage is not the absence of fear, but rather moving ahead in spite of our fears. I allowed my fear to so grip my thinking that I took a less than favorable approach.

Second, I was not honest with my friend John by withholding the truth about how I was handling his request. I left him assuming that I was proceeding with his request in the manner that he had asked me to, but all the while, I was not. Instead, I approached the comptroller and bluntly shared with him as my best friend what John had asked me to do, which did two unfortunate things. First, it put the comptroller in the awkward position of having to deal with the problem that I had failed to address. Second, my action also cast a question mark over the character of my friend John, and he did not know about it until several years later when I talked to him about my actions and sought his forgiveness.

In the course of life, each of us likely will be confronted with ethical dilemmas and be called upon to respond properly. In short, we should simply do what is right and, in the process, speak the truth out of humility and love, doing so to the right people at the right time. When fear first manifests itself, we must also be prepared to move against our fears with a determination to do right regardless of the consequences. As the old Southern evangelist, Bob Jones Sr. used to say, "Do right! Do right if the stars fall!" I can still hear him saying, "Girls and boys, when you do wrong, even in order to get a chance to do right, you're not doing right when you think you're doing right!"

The fact that we live in a fallen world of sinful human beings means that we will periodically feel the sting of disappointments from those around us, whether friends, associates, relatives, neighbors, or superiors.

That's life. It's going to happen numerous times in our lives. Although it never "feels good" while we're experiencing it, as we act and respond properly, we can maintain a calm confidence and inner strength that comes only from proper actions on our part. And the harsh reality is that we will experience such events periodically throughout our lives.

Chewed out by a trusted friend

While serving as the senior pastor in a distant city and state, I was enjoying the consistent growth of the church. That's always exciting. Adding to the excitement was the fact that many of the men who were joining our congregation were becoming very dear friends to me. It has never been my personal practice to avoid building friendships with the people of the churches where I have served. Although I've heard preachers advise that a pastor should never get too close to his people or they will lose respect for him as their pastor, I've always wondered what kind of life those guys were living that would cause a congregant to lose respect for them as they became better acquainted! Besides, if we're to follow the example of Jesus Christ, we must get close to other people, especially those men whom we would mentor. After all, one of the names of Christ—Emmanuel—means "God with us." He spent much time traveling with, eating with, and talking with those who would follow Him. To get close to others, we must be willing to run the risk of being hurt.

For example, as I was studying for my Wednesday evening talk to an adult group at the church, the secretary, who was on her way out the door for the rest of the day, informed me that I had a call on line two, and that she would see me again that evening at the service. When I answered the telephone, I discovered that one of the finest men in the congregation and a very dear friend was on the line. The man, an independent contractor from the construction industry, and I had been very close and often spent several minutes talking about ministry and the scriptures following services. He had been a generous donor and served wherever he could in the ministries of the church and Christian school that we operated—and he did so selflessly. He asked if he could come to the office to see me.

A half hour later, he arrived at the church office complex. As he came into my office, he closed and locked the door, walked across the room, and sat down on the couch near my desk without saying a word. This unusual behavior certainly arrested my attention, but I was clueless to what I was about to hear. From the legal pad on his lap, my trusted friend and board member unloaded a freight train of complaints—more than three legal pages full of notes. I listened and asked questions. He had come to make his case. There were many things that were "wrong" with me, with my family, with my leadership, and with the congregation. For more than three hours, my friend worked his way through the prepared list. When he was finished and confirmed for me that he had nothing else on his mind, I asked if I could close our meeting in prayer. He agreed, I prayed a simple, brief prayer, and he said goodbye and left—not just the office, but the church.

When he had left, I locked the lobby and office doors, retreated to my office, and sat for several minutes in silence. I was devastated. I felt as though I had been strung up and field dressed alive. I'd just been "gutted" by a friend. It felt like an ambush. I wept. I prayed. I contemplated what to do next. In just two hours I would have to stand and address an audience and be the on-point pastor that the congregation had come to expect. A root canal without anesthesia would have been less painful.

I considered contacting my informal advisory board of mentors, but, one by one, I dismissed the idea of contacting them, in part because I couldn't imagine admitting to any of them that I had allowed a man to attack me verbally for three hours. But I needed to talk to a seasoned minister who would understand and give me the encouragement and advice that I might need to get through that evening's service and for the next few days or weeks. It dawned on me that my father's pastor, Dr. Harold Clayton, back in Tennessee had been through a few difficulties of his own. He accepted my phone call at his home and spent several minutes encouraging, reassuring, and valuing me. I remember his advice to this day.

Although I have never forgotten the hurt of that Wednesday afternoon and the great quantity of unjust criticism, I was able to work past it and forgive and release the friend who had virtually destroyed our friendship. However, that isn't how the story ends.

Eight years later, as I left my office in Davisburg, Michigan, the phone rang. The secretaries were at lunch, and I was on my way to a lunch appointment as well, but thinking perhaps it could be an emergency, I answered the ringing phone. "Good afternoon, First Baptist Church of Davisburg." On the other end of the line was a familiar, soft-spoken male voice. It was that of my independent contractor friend hundreds of miles away! I was thrilled to hear from him after so many years.

After briefing me on his family and business, he slowly said, "Preacher, I'm sure you're really busy, so I'll try to be brief." He shared with me how, after teaching his adult Sunday school class the day before, a man came to him and spent five minutes criticizing him for something he had said during the class. "Preacher," he said, "I went to the morning service, but I was so hurt and angry that I didn't hear anything that was said or sung. As we drove home, I told [my wife] about the criticism and the hurt. At the lunch table, I told [my wife], 'That must be a little taste of what it's like to be a pastor. In fact, I remember doing that to a pastor about eight years ago—only it was for three hours, not just five minutes.'" According to my friend, his spouse's response was simply, "Well, what are you going to do about it?"

By that point in his explanation, I was standing in the front office weeping—for the pain that my friend had experienced, for the courage that he had exhibited in calling me within twenty-four hours of his conversation with his wife, and for the humility and tenderness that I heard in his voice. "Preacher, could you find it in your heart to forgive me for being so brutal with you years ago?"

Has someone wronged you or spoken critically of you? Can you find it in your heart to forgive them— even before they ask? I know, I know. Some readers are already thinking, *I'm not going to forgive them until they ask me!* Oh, my friend, you then run the risk of becoming an increasingly bitter person and damaging yourself. That doesn't sound very healthy. Besides, it doesn't sound like the example set by Jesus Christ either. Do you remember how He responded to those who had wronged Him? "Father, forgive them for they know not what they do," and those words were uttered agonizingly through parched and swollen lips from the cross where He would die a few minutes later.

Do you want to be like Christ? Learn to forgive, and do so quickly and deliberately.

Set up for the ambush by trusted board members

The board meetings had increasingly become antag-onistic, but I could not put my finger on any specific issues that might be precipitating the undercurrent of discontent among some of the board members each month. After about three monthly meetings like that, everything seemed to come to a head—and it became personal in a hurry. On the seven-member board, at least three men had become quite vocally critical, and a fourth was ramping it up. The other three sat rather silently around the conference table.

With twenty years of pastoral experience already under my belt, I had gained confidence in handling controversy, so in that particular meeting it had become obvious that at least half the board had collaborated and had come with a laundry list of criticism. Not only did I listen and ask questions that evening but also I took excellent notes on what was being stated and who was bringing it to the table. That Monday night meeting went past midnight, and although I thought that some of the grievances were laughable, I treated everything as seri-ously as a Supreme Court justice. When the critics had wound down, someone suggested that they give me the opportunity to respond, noting that I had said nothing in my own defense.

I agreed that I would like the opportunity to address the issues that had been raised. "But not tonight," I replied. "It's almost 1:00 A.M., and everyone is tired. Knowing how important these issues are to you gentlemen, I would like for us to resume our meeting tomorrow night at 7:00 P.M. here in the boardroom, and I will respond at that time."

One gentleman rather piously responded, "I'm sure that you would like time to pray over these issues before you respond." I must admit that my own sarcastic thoughts were more along the line of *No, I just want to get out of here before I snap and choke someone!* Everyone agreed to adjourn until 7:00 P.M. the next night, someone closed the meeting with a prayer, and we adjourned.

The following evening, after an opening prayer, the chairman of the board yielded the floor for my response. I began by thanking the men for their forthrightness, acknowledging that it must not have been easy for them to confront their pastor with all of those issues. After reassuring them that I took each accusation very seriously, I outlined what I would like for us to do in that particular meeting. We agreed to cover each item as it had been presented the night before, and I wanted to ask questions and restate each criticism in my own words to ensure that I had clearly understood the issues. Next, we would go back to each item in the sequence in which they originally had been presented and discuss and agree to a solution that should reasonably resolve each issue. Additionally, I stated that we would also attach names to each item so that we knew with whom I would be resolving the conflicts.

At that point, the three main critics on the board balked, stating, "These people are our friends. They have taken us into their confidence. We can't do that."

This opened the door for me to firmly address a critical issue—the reality that they had just confirmed that they neither understood the biblical process for resolving conflicts nor were they being honest about wanting to resolve the conflicts. "While some of these people may be your friends," I said, "they are all the members of my congregation, and if there is truly a problem, no one in the room wants to work toward a solution more than I do. And, gentlemen, if you are unwilling to name the people who have raised the issues, I must assume that it is *you* who really has the problem, and we will then deal with not only the supposed problem but also your lack of honesty. Have I made myself clear?" The room was deathly quiet. "Then we can continue now with the process," I stated.

The third step was to set up a schedule of appointments with each member who had been identified in the meeting as having taken offense or having had a concern with a particular issue or multiple issues, and I would take one of the board members with me to make a personal visit in each home and to witness that I indeed did the things that we had agreed would reasonably solve each difficulty. What I did not tell the board members was that I was planning to take the member with me who had brought the offense of another member to me.

We began the process shortly after the meeting began, but approaching midnight, we had hardly scratched the surface. We agreed to adjourn until 7:00 P.M. the next evening. Again, I emphasized to the men the urgency that I felt in solving each accusation with the members.

When the meeting was called to order the next evening and someone had prayed, the chairman stated, "Some of us have been talking and we don't think it is necessary for us to discuss every detail." I cut him off with the sternness of an NFL coach going to the locker room at half time with his team trailing by two touchdowns. "Gentlemen, you brought these issues to the table and said that they were serious problems. Understand that I intend to deal with every one of them fully." "Now, let's go to work right where we left off last night!"

Do you remember the earlier fear that had griped my mind when it came to dealing opening, honestly, and humbly with people problems? Have you now noticed a change in the mindset that I employed? What made the difference? In brief, I had learned to move against my fears. However, that isn't the most important issue for our consideration. The issue at hand is how we handle the hurts and disappointments of life when they come from friends.

First, we must be willing to listen objectively even to those who are critical. Although we live in a culture of self-expression, it seems to me that if everyone is *talking*, then no one is *listening*. If we can discipline ourselves truly to listen to what others are saying, we can learn a great deal more than when we are talking or thinking about what we want to say next.

Second, we must exercise wisdom as we consider the validity (in this case) of the criticism. Not every criticism will be accurate, but some of them will be close enough to the truth that, if we are truly and honestly listening, we can gain insights into areas in our lives that are weak or misguided and need attention and improvement.

Third, we must be prepared to take appropriate action when we recognize that a dimension of our attitudes, actions, conversations, or operations is deficit or off base. At times, our critics might have rotten attitudes toward us or use inappropriate methods or words in getting their points across to us, but that does not invalidate the truth of what they might present to us.

We read about the rebellion of Absalom, son of King David, in 2 Samuel. Wearied from previous battles and no doubt emotionally drained from both the military involvements and the treacherous behavior of Absalom, the king, to avoid a battle in the revolt of his own son, fled from Jerusalem. As David and a host of people were seeking a place to rest, Shemei, a relative of King Saul and a critic of King David, came to where David was and cursed him and threw stones at him. When the king's companions suggested that he allow them to put a stop to Shemei's verbal ranting and physical attacks, David instructed them to leave Shemei alone. David even contemplated the possibility that God could be using legitimately the critic to accomplish something in the life of the king. However, David did not stop with that possibility, but responded in the typical fashion of David. He threw himself on the mercy of the Lord, saying, "It may be that the Lord will look on mine affliction, and that the Lord will requite me good for his cursing this day" (2 Samuel 16:12).

In our modern culture, with its various forms of "getting even" for wrongs perpetrated against us, one of which the least is law suits for every frivolous thing, it is a rarity to find individuals, even among supposed Christ-followers. who respond after the manner of King David. We should ever be mindful that it was Jesus Christ himself who gave us in the Sermon on the Mount rock-solid instructions for handling those who hurt or wrong us.

"Love your enemies, bless them that curse you, do good to them that hate you, and pray for them which despitefully use you, and persecute you" (Matthew 5:44).

Returning to the malicious board members who were (figuratively) cursing me, the ringleader and negative influence, who also happened to be the chairman of the board at the time, abruptly resigned his position on the board, as did two of the remaining board members who were his cohorts. But they were not of a mind to give up so easily, having really lost face among the other members of the board. Besides, I was still the pastor, and that was not what they had bargained for. Apparently, they assumed that heaping on that much discouragement at one time would force my resignation. That strategy had failed, so they retreated to their hangout, the local volunteer fire department, to develop plan "B."

Within a few weeks, the church held its regular quarterly business meeting. It had been a rather benign, uneventful meeting of rather routine reports and other business—until I called for a motion to adjourn. At that point, the former chairman of the board stood and moved that the church request the pastor's resignation and, if I should refuse, that the pastor be terminated immediately. I could hardly believe my ears, and it was so ludicrous that it almost seemed comical, except that it was serious unannounced business.

I looked in disbelief at the congregation, and said, "Well, folks, we have a motion on the floor. That will require a second before we can proceed." Almost instantly, another board member jokingly said, "It will never get a second!"

However, one of the good ol' boys from the local volunteer fire department sneeringly said, "Oh yeah? I'll second that motion."

Almost everyone in attendance was in disbelief, stunned by the words just spoken and their significance. Before proceeding further with the business at hand, but not before being interrupted by the man who made the motion, I asked a former board chairman and current member of our board, Dick Mills, treasurer for SEND International, a missionary agency in Farmington Hills, Michigan, to come forward to the podium and assume the moderator's role as I yielded to him. Although I had no clue what he would do, I knew that he was quite capable of handling a difficult circumstance like this. He did not disappoint.

His first instructions and admonitions could not have been better if I had scripted it myself. He stated clearly several critical guidelines for the discussion. First, he said that the motion on the floor did not represent the board and certainly did not represent his personal views but simply the opinions of two members of the church. Second, he let the audience know that the discussion would not be allowed to get out of hand, become a lynching of the pastor, or go on indefinitely. He then asked how long the members would like to discuss the motion. Someone jokingly quipped, "Oh, I think about two minutes ought to be long enough," but the acting moderator quickly reinforced the seriousness of the moment. The members agreed to limit the discussion to thirty minutes. At the end of the discussion, they voted to table the motion , and a special business meeting was scheduled for two weeks later, at which time the issues surrounding the motion would be discussed and a vote taken.

Whether the timing of all of that was good or bad, I'm still not sure, but the next morning my family and I left for a two-week vacation on the beach in North Carolina. Although I tried not to be consumed with thoughts of the pending special business meeting, I failed miserably. It seemed to be all I could think about. I went through the motions of the vacation, but my mind was completely preoccupied. Thankfully, my wife made the vacation exciting for herself and the kids, and we returned to the dreaded meeting two weeks later.

The board had met and agreed to allow the man who had made the motion to present his reasoning, then allow a time for questions and answers from the congregation. Following that, I could present my perspective, followed by another Q&A session. When the acting moderator told me the plan, I agreed that it was a good approach; however, "Other than a brief, written statement, I told him, I have nothing to say." When he asked about the possibility of answering questions, I agreed to answer any questions that either he as the acting moderator or the congregation could not answer adequately.

The next evening, as my wife and I entered the auditorium and sat together about half way back the center aisle, I calmly quipped, "This is kind of neat! We never get to sit together in church!" With a bewildered look in my direction, she asked, "Oh how can you joke at a time like this?" It was at that moment that I was aware that I was at perfect peace, and I wondered for a moment why I could not have enjoyed that peace back at the beach in North Carolina for two weeks! But then the meeting was called to order.

The tall gentleman who originally had made the motion was introduced and began a rambling verbal presentation of why he felt compelled to make such a motion. Within a few moments, I began actually to feel sorry for the poor fellow. The longer he talked, the deeper he dug himself into a hole. Soon, hands began to go into the air, as individuals awaited their opportunity to ask questions. Throughout the discussion, I did not speak a single word in self- defense. It was unnecessary. The congregation as a whole could not begin to identify with either the man or his motion. At least in my mind, the classic statement of the entire evening came from the oldest gentleman in the church, Clare Brown, a godly man from Holly, Michigan, whom I still miss to this day. Grasping the back of the pew in front of him for support, he slowly rose to his feet and quietly and graciously said, "I can't help but believe that if we had this kind of crowd out for prayer meetings and praying together on Wednesday nights, we wouldn't be having this kind of meeting tonight," and then slowly seated himself again. Profound words.

The moderator finally turned to me and said, "Pastor, we have done all the talking tonight. Is there anything that you would like to say before we cast our votes?" While I do not recall what I said, it was a brief, scripted note that I read, and then I returned to my seat. When the secret ballots were counted, only eleven people—a very small percentage of the congregation—voted in favor of the motion. Although I had accepted a 97 percent vote to become the pastor of the church two years earlier, I realized that practically speaking, that night I truly became the pastor of the church.

By this point you are probably wondering how I handled those who voted in favor of the motion. Did I retaliate? Actually, I never really knew who those eleven people were, and I never wasted mental energy worrying about it. The opinions of a few people had clearly been overridden by the will of the many. However, within the next few weeks, a few constituents left the church—but not eleven voting members, and not the gentleman who had made the original motion, although the man who seconded the motion did so. Did that bother me?

While I could never understand why someone so opposed to my leadership would continue his membership in the church, he chose to stay—and I chose to love him because that's what Christians and pastors of God's people are supposed to do. Was it always easy to love someone who had tried to hurt my family and me? No, it was not always easy, but I can honestly say that, to this very day, I still love that man as a Christian brother. During my remaining years as the pastor, he came often enough at least to meet the minimum constitutional attendance requirements for active membership, put his head in his hands, with elbows on his knees, and looked at the floor, or looked away, for the duration of every sermon I delivered. Whether he listened, I do not know, but what I do know is that I accepted a critical teaching of Jesus' Sermon on the Mount as my goal in relating to him.

"But I say unto you, Love your enemies, bless them that curse you, do good to them that hate you, and pray for them which despitefully use you, and persecute you (Matthew 5:44). The gospel of Luke records Jesus' words thus: "Bless them that curse you, and pray for them which despitefully use you (Luke 6:28).

Abandoned by trusted friends in time of crisis

The volume of questions had continued to grow for several months before two wonderful ladies from my congregation approached me with troubling discoveries they had made concerning personal family matters of which I was unaware. Their honesty with me was painful for each of them and for me, and each of them later conveyed a hint of regret for giving me heart-breaking news, and yet without that information from those whom I could trust, I would later have been blind-sided by that which seemed inevitable.

A few months later, my whole world came crashing down as my wife of thirty years walked out, thus creating a difficult circumstance for a pastor. My board was at best divided over whether I should continue as their pastor, given that my spouse had left our home and our marriage seemed to be heading for divorce. Because I understood the hurt and distrust that infidelity can inflict on a church's membership, and having to earn a congregation's trust after a previous pastor had betrayed their confidence, I knew that I did not want them to be thrust unduly into another similar scenario. I had already assured the board that I would not do that. However, the logic and reaction of the board is something that escapes me to this day.

Most of the advice that I received from pastor friends from around the world was not to resign or not to resign too hastily. Their advice usually included a statement such as, "You have been there for your people, now let them be there for you."

In retrospect, the people within the church responded in one of three ways. First, some members came along side and were *there* for me from the very moment they learned of what was happening. Most of the people in that group knew the pain of divorce and came to my rescue any way they could, and their expressions of love and concern astounded me. The second group of people was members and friends who truly loved my family and me but were not personally close and were no doubt uncertain what, if anything, they could say or do.

But it was the third group that caused great anguish—those with whom I had the closest relationships and had spent the greatest amounts of time as fellow laborers. In time, as the opportunities arose, I asked three board members with whom I had been especially close, "Where were you guys? I was going through the longest, darkest, loneliest valley of my life, and you were nowhere to be found!" Rather lamely, I thought, each responded basically the same way: "Pastor, we didn't know what to say or do."

What I have never understood is this—and this is something that everyone can benefit from if we choose to do so—how, then, did they conclude that the right thing to say or do was *nothing*?

In the course of life as a minister, many times I was in a position where I did not know what to say or do. For example, when I stood with my arms around young parents who had just lost an infant in the emergency room and felt so helpless and heartbroken that all I could do was weep with them. Sitting in the home with a family whose husband and father was dying within minutes, I didn't know what I could say that was adequate to meet their need, and the thought of my own helplessness and their pending loss caused an eruption of my own tears that mingled with theirs. But one thing was never in question—I could love them and *be there* with them in their times of loss or need.

Made the scapegoat by trusted peers

From time to time in life, each of us will be hurt by the attitudes, actions, or articulations of the people around us—and the hurt is very real. However, when those wounds come from family, trusted friends, or peers, the pain is intensified many times over. Such was the case for me just a few years ago.

After enduring the heartache and turmoil surrounding my resignation from the church of which I was the pastor, relocating two teenage children and myself from a nice, large home into a small mother-in-law apartment, changing jobs three times in as many years, and trying to rebound from a divorce, my life as a father and a minister was beginning to find fresh direction and energy. Life was beginning to *look up* again.

But, remember how I wrote earlier that we're either in a storm or valley, just coming out of a personal storm or valley, or about to discover another storm or valley? I was about to discover once again the reality of my own analysis of life!

The days of real estate appraising and representing a dot.com company as vice-president of my division were behind me. Although I continued to speak itinerantly, the income was not always consistent and sufficient to support a family, so I had accepted a position on the support staff of the church that my children and

I now called "home." My primary responsibilities were ensuring that the building complex was clean, repaired, and properly set for the various functions and ministries that took place each week.

Those responsibilities might have occupied much of my daily time, but it was the ministry functions such as teaching the Cornerstone Class of young married couples, preaching, and counseling that still occupied my heart and motivated me toward the future. Our church was struggling with a long, slow decline in attendance (and subsequently offerings). Opinions and tensions abounded, although they were generally kept under the radar. The frustrations were real and growing.

Even my dear pastor friend came to my office at the church one afternoon, closed the door behind him, sat on the couch along the side wall, and after a dramatic pause, asked, "Dale, is it time for me to leave?" I was stunned at the abruptness of his question but not the reality of his question. One cannot pastor for as many years as I have and not understand some of the pressure and stress that my friend was facing. Until that question, my pastor and I had not discussed the growing situation.

My response drew upon my own years of pastoral experience. "Pastor, having made that decision more than once, and knowing the difficulty of making that determination, why would I presume to answer that question for another man?" was my bewildered reply. After a few minutes of discussion concerning what was behind the abrupt question, we parted company, never to discuss it further. However, not many weeks later, my friend of at least a decade announced his resignation, and upon its effect, left a historic church devoid of leadership, at least at the board level, of vision and wisdom in sufficient quantity to bring the ship-of-state back from decline and onto a course of growth and spiritual vitality.

It was my opinion that, with the existing staff at that time, there was adequate pastoral input to stabilize the diminutive congregation and lead a healthy transition until such time as a new senior pastor could be brought onto the scene. However, rather than accepting the insights offered by the three experienced pastors on staff, the board at best used the three of us as "pulpit supply," while they were drowning in despair. The divisions in-house were enough to drive a leader or leadership team with direction, passion, and vision to the brink of insanity, but for a board lacking in those same elements, it was overwhelming.

Although I eventually spoke in favor of the course of action that the board presented to the congregation, the idea of a merger was never my first choice. To this day, I still believe that a revival of that historic church (the oldest Baptist church in Michigan and with a glorious track record of effectiveness for God through the years) was the greatest option. However, to exercise that *option* would absolutely require solid leadership that was unwavering on four critical elements—value, vision, passion, and program.

Rather than pursuing a course of action to recapture what the church had historically possessed but had lost somewhere along the way, the idea (and offer) of a merger with a larger, thriving church was presented. As trial balloons were being released, reflecting the direction of the board's thinking, I came to a point of realization that unless something dramatic took place quickly, the church would soon die an embarrassing and public death; therefore, a merger represented the quickest possible turnaround.

During a conversation with my friend Jeff Totten, chaplain for the Detroit Tigers, and then interim pastor of the church, I stated it was my belief that a merger would afford the congregation the quickest possible turnaround. Jeff asked if I would be willing to "put that in writing." Within hours, I fired off an email to Jeff stating, for the record that very idea. It was used regularly over the next few months as a "selling point" for the merger, especially to influence those among the congregation who had expressed strong feelings that I should be called as the senior pastor, or at least given the responsibility of interim pastor—neither of which I had sought.

Eventually, we conducted perhaps the most critical business meeting in the church's century-plus history, and a congregation of less than 200 members voted to give approximately eleven million dollars of assets to another church that knew what to do with it—all my opinion, of course. More sadly to me than watching that church's history end in a merger would have been to witness its eventual death by default.

But other disheartening events surrounded those days—events that affected me at the personal level.

Bringing more than twenty years of ministry experience as a senior pastor to the table, although I was not serving with the title as an associate pastor but rather on the support staff and fulfilling numerous pastoral responsibilities, I at times found myself in awkward positions, feeling caught between my previous ministry track record and my actual role at the church. While my pastoral experience could have been of great value to a church in decline, that seemed to be obscured by my actual position on the support staff.

Because I brought valuable pulpit experience with me, the board tapped me to help cover approximately 75 percent of the preaching responsibilities—two Sunday mornings each month and all the Sunday evening services. However, even that divided the congregation, with a growing delegation of members who liked what they were hearing from the pulpit and those who, for whatever reasons unknown to me, felt that another direction and another person should be considered.

On numerous days, I felt like Rodney King, the African-American who was videotaped receiving an over-the-top beating by law enforcement officers in Los Angeles on March 3, 1991: "Can't we all just get along?!"

Not only was there a growing concern that became increasingly heavy upon my heart and mind but also the continual malaise of discontent among the congregants. But I must tell you, God is still on His throne even in our darkest days and most bleak circumstances. As the songwriter penned, "It's always darkest before the dawn; don't be discouraged, but carry on." And God, in His perfect timing, was about to burst into my despondent world once again with fresh new direction!

Ministerial friends from across the country were coming to a national conference of the Baptist Bible Fellowship, hosted by the Beacon Baptist Church of Taylor, Michigan, and my long-time friend Herb Gilbert. Several of us met together for dinner in Greektown (downtown Detroit) and returned in time to attend the closing service that Tuesday evening.

While crossing the lobby, I heard my name called and turned into a big bear hug from my friend Dr. Leland Kennedy, retired president of Baptist Bible College in Springfield, Missouri. "Dale, we were just talking about you two days ago over in Ireland!" he exclaimed

"We *who*?" I replied. "Tom Wallace Sr.," Dr. Kennedy responded.

Two thoughts immediately and simultaneously traced their courses through my mind. First, why would my name come up in a conversation between those two friends in Ireland? I had not seen or talked to Tom since the late 1970s and only crossed paths with Leland a couple of times a year somewhere in America, usually at a conference similar to that one.

The second thought was an instantaneous silent prayer. "Lord, I don't know what you're saying, but I'm listening!" Somehow, I knew in my soul that this was a God moment. In explainable terms, I knew that the direction of my life and ministry was about to change— and it was change we could believe in!

Dr. Kennedy described how he and Tom Wallace were discussing the spiritual condition of the United Kingdom, and Tom reminisced, "You know, about 25 years ago [it was 27 years earlier to be exact], a black-haired young man named Dale Peterson came to Great Britain. Dale preached and a team of singers [the SMITE (Student Missionary Intern Training for Evangelism) Singers, a missions oriented team of students from Liberty Baptist College] sang. Many of our churches had revival—but we didn't keep it going."

As my retired college president friend spoke, my heart opened to God's leadership, and somehow I knew that God was redirecting my ministry toward Europe. Although I spoke of that to no one right away, I could not get that conversation off my mind. Dr. Kennedy and I shared several telephone conversations together over the next few weeks. One morning several weeks later, our mutual friend and mentor Dr. John Rawlings called me and began telling me God's plan for the rest if my life. Those who know Dr. John well understand that statement, a bit tongue-in-cheek but packed with a lot of truth. I even heard Dr. Jerry Falwell say at Mrs. Orelia Rawlings's funeral that Dr. John called him every day and told him what God's plan for his life was that day.

Today, as I write these words, I'm sitting in my room in the chateau outside Brussels, having just participated in a think-tank conference of ministers whose focus is on the United Kingdom and Europe, brainstorming how we can refine our focus for more effective ministry and develop systems to accomplish those goals. It is phenomenal when God works—especially as He guides our steps through the valleys of life!

What difficulty are you facing now? Does a struggle in your life leave you despondent and discouraged? Oscar C. Eliason certainly penned words of encouragement when he wrote,

> *Got any rivers you think are uncrossable?*
> *Got any mountains you can't tunnel through?*
> *God specializes in things thought impossible.*
> *He'll do for you what no other friend can do!*

My friend, your current valley is no surprise to the God who wants to direct your every step and accomplish in and through you exceeding abundantly more than you're able to think or ask! Trust Him! Determine at this very moment that you will not merely survive this time of testing but will thrive through it! And although your thriving does not depend on your own strength or wisdom, it will be contingent upon your deciding to look beyond that present hardship or trial.

> *That the trial of your faith, being much more precious than of gold that perisheth, though it be tried with fire, might be found unto praise*

and honour and glory at the appearing of Jesus Chris. (1 Peter 1:7)

If you will choose now to trust Him in the valley of your life, you can find renewed empowerment to

Leave a well in the valley, the dark and lonesome valley;
Others have to cross this valley, too:
And what a blessing when they find the well of joy
you've left behind,
So, leave a well in the valley you go through.

Scriptures on Which to Meditate

(John 16:33 New Living Translation)

I have told you all this so that you may have peace in me. Here on earth you will have many trials and sorrows. But take heart, because I have overcome the world."

(Romans 5:3–5a NCV)

We also have joy with our troubles, because we know that these troubles produce patience. And patience produces character, and character produces hope. And this hope will never disappoint us, because God has poured out his love to fill our hearts.

(1 Peter 1:6–7 GWT)

You are extremely happy about these things, even though you have to suffer different kinds of trouble for a little while now. The purpose of these troubles is to test your faith as fire tests how genuine gold is. Your faith is more precious than gold, and by passing the test, it gives praise, glory, and honor to God. This will happen when Jesus Christ appears again.

(1 Peter 5:6-7 KJV)

Humble yourselves therefore under the mighty hand of God, that he may exalt you in due time: Casting all your care upon him; for he careth for you.

(1 Peter 5:10-11 KJV)

But the God of all grace, who hath called us unto his eternal glory by Christ Jesus, after that ye have suffered a while, make you perfect, stablish, strengthen, settle you. To him be glory and dominion for ever and ever. Amen.

10

When It's All Said and Done

To someone driving a car that goes into a skid, the advice is to "steer in the direction of the skid." The inexperienced driver thinks that is the most illogical advice one could receive—until that driver finds himself in a skid. In the few nanoseconds required to process what is happening and respond, if the driver will steer into the skid, the odds improve for correcting the automobile's trajectory and avoiding an accident.

To a tired swimmer in trouble, the natural reaction is one of panic; yet, that is the worst possible response. What one needs in a time of crisis is calmness and presence of mind to relax, remember the simple instructions from bygone swimming lessons—to flip over on your back and float or to tread water.

In a water rescue of a swimmer in panic, the natural action might be to approach them from a direction that allows the troubled swimmer to see that help is moments away; yet, the better approach is from behind them, lest in his panicked state of mind he grasps and flails at the rescuer, hindering the rescue process.

Similar events happen all along the road of life as we journey from cradle to grave. Many voices in our world give advice on every imaginable subject. After six decades of life experiences and forty years of ministry experience, I'm shocked by very little anymore concerning the kind of advice that is available today. However, only a few days ago I *was* surprised when a pastor friend from the New England area pointed my attention to a website for "Christian nymphomaniacs!" As extreme as that sounds to many of us, advice is apparently being freely distributed even on *that* subject and a host of others equally bizarre, at least to *my* way of thinking.

With so many kinds of voices calling for our time and attention, to whom should we listen? When we are uncertain and need direction, where should we turn to find reliable advice?

In 1993, Dr. James Dobson was the Commencement speaker at the graduation of my oldest daughter Charity at Liberty University. He arrested my attention as he recounted a personal story about a visit that he made to his alma mater in southern California some years after his graduation from college. He spoke of the trophies that he had won as a collegiate tennis star and the display cases in the corridors and lobby of the athletic buildings. Visiting an old professor friend one day, he was forced to park in an obscure spot near a rubbish dumpster. Something protruding from the commercial dumpster and glistening in the sun caught his attention. Upon investigating, he discovered that hundreds of trophies had been discarded, including dozens that *he* had won during his collegiate years.

During his address to my daughter's graduating class, Dr. Dobson first spoke of the concept that the world will "trash your trophies" but continued with the admonition to do things with their lives that would outlive them. In fact, he encouraged the audience of well-over 10,000 people to (in their minds) go out to the cemetery where a grave had been dug for their caskets, sit on the edge of the open six-foot-deep hole with their legs dangling in it, and contemplate what they would like for those who would one day gather for their funeral to say truthfully about them when the time came. Then he told them to come back to that moment of graduation and determine to live in such a way as to bring those good things to pass.

That isn't to say that everything in life is easy, will go our way, or will always turn out the way we want them to end. However, it is certainly a favorable manner in which we can help ourselves identify and determine objectives, set goals, and live our lives. We must make our plans, counting on God to direct our steps. The wise man wrote, "We can make our plans, but the LORD determines our steps" (Prov. 16:9 NLT).

None of us will traverse the journey of life without trials, burdens, setbacks, failures, and disappointments. Some of them will be because we make honest mistakes. Others will be results of a direct or indirect failure by us or someone else. Still others might overtake us without human explanation. So, when it's all said and done, how can we face forward and plunge with excitement and determination into our futures?

First, we must remember that we are weak, but He is strong. Therefore, during those times when our weaknesses seem to overshadow our strengths, we must *depend on* Him.

Sometimes the answers to our questions and the supply for our needs can be found in the simplicities or the basics of life. Oh how often we could find relief from our worries and solace from our fears by singing the old children's song "Jesus Loves Me" and applying the words and principles to our lives!

> *Jesus loves me, this I know;*
> *For the Bible tells me so.*
> *Little ones to Him belong;*
> *They are weak, but He is strong.*

A popular song of encouragement and inspiration a few years ago used the phrase *You are the wind beneath my wings.* Just as a bird or a sailboat must depend upon the wind, so we must depend upon God—for everything. When we neglect to acknowledge that we are totally dependent upon the Lord, we begin a vulnerability from within that will lead us into one of life's classrooms where we must repeat the lesson of utter dependence upon the One who created us.

Regrettably, many people are unaware of their need for dependence. Still others might declare that they are self-made men or women and, in doing so, declare that they do not need God, even cursing Him. However, whether through defiance or ignorance, they *are* dependent upon him for their every heartbeat and must get the very breath with which they curse God from the air that He has made.

While journeying along the road of life, we are dependent upon Him for all things, regardless of whether we are aware of or acknowledge this reality. Therefore, we should also *trust* Him.

Have you ever experienced in which you have stated something to a friend or relative and then received in response a look of skepticism? They just aren't sure if you know what you're talking about. It's then common to say, "Trust me—I know what I'm talking about!" Surely that's how God must look at us!

My Lord knows the way through the wilderness; all I have to do is follow!

I don't know about tomorrow, I just live from day to day.

The bottom line is that neither you nor I really has a clue what the next minute of life holds for us, do we? The residents of Port-au-Prince, Haiti, were going about their lives—business as usual—in January 2010 when a 7.0 earthquake flattened their city, killing tens of thousands of people. Nightly newscasts reflect horrible automobile crashes that claimed the lives of untold numbers of victims around the world—people who were just going about their routine lives without a clue that this day could be their last day on earth—that their next breath could be their last. As Jesus stated,

But God said unto him, *Thou* fool, this night thy soul shall be required of thee: then whose shall those things be, which thou hast provided? [21]So *is* he that layeth up treasure for himself, and is not rich toward God. (Luke 12:20-21)

Although we might not have a clue what awaits us around the next curve on the road of life, we can know and trust the One who knows every detail, including the very number of hairs on our heads (Matt 10:30). And if Jesus Christ is interested enough in you and me to know *that* kind of detail about our lives, shouldn't we cultivate the relationship with and trust Him?

This leads me to a third thought—*know* Him. You see, there is nothing about you that He doesn't know and understand. Before you were formed in your mother's womb, God knew every detail of your life. No joy or sorrow has escaped His attention. Every happiness and heartache He has felt. As one songwriter penned so well, you matter so much to Jesus Christ, that we can each say,

When He was on the cross, I was on His mind!

But while He knows every thought and intent of our hearts and the details of our lives, there is so much about Him that we don't know—which is why it is important that we get to *know* Him.

Life lived for self becomes empty and meaningless; but life lived for Christ becomes fruitful and fulfilling Live for Him. Periodically, I encounter individuals who are skeptical or afraid to yield their lives to God, people who think, "If I tell God that I'll do whatever He wants me to do or go wherever He wants me to go, I'll have to spend the rest of my life miserable!"

Nothing could be further from the truth! The emptiness and dissatisfaction that comes when we turn to our own way, like sheep gone astray, creates far more misery than being what God wants us to be, doing what He wants us to do, and going where He might lead us.

The greatest fulfillment in life can be found only in total obedience to His gracious leading.

Many days in the course of a lifetime might become lonely, but He is always there for you. *Talk* to Him.

Many people in this world live for themselves alone. However, the child of God, the follower of Christ, is called upon to live beyond self, to die to self and live for others. Therefore, we are called to *serve* Him.

The world's boast, as the famous song recorded by Frank Sinatra says, is "I Did It My Way" with an independent spirit; but we were meant to complement each other. Let's serve Him *together*! For decades now, whether traveling nationally or internationally, I'm confronted with the recurring spirit of independence among believers.

I stepped off a Pan-Am flight to Manila years ago. I was on a strategic trip to plan for a national pastors and Christian workers conference at the then newly constructed Philippine Plaza Hotel and International Convention Centre. After a limousine whisked me from the airport to my hotel room at the official hotel of the conference, a key leader of a Baptist organization with which I had been affiliated for years met me. The first question he asked was, "Now, Dale, this is just going to be our group, correct?" My heart was grieved instantly.

Although I am by no means an ecumenist, willing to bring all faiths together, I am thoroughly convinced that the work of God has been hindered severely by the unwillingness of many Christian leaders truly to embrace the major, fundamental doctrines that bring us into the family of God and to look beyond the things of lesser importance—things that often divide—and work together to accomplish greater things for our Lord Jesus Christ. Somehow, we overlook such simple commands as

When we have the opportunity to help anyone, we should do it. But we should give special attention to those who are in the family of believers. (Gal 6:10 NCV)

A selfish world demands to receive for themselves, but having been blessed abundantly already by our loving, generous Heavenly Father, *give* to Him. This becomes a natural outworking of our authentic love for the Lord, as well as our love for those for whom He gave His life two thousand years ago on Calvary. Doing good will always require that we give up something of self, but it is never really a sacrifice. Rather, it is a guaranteed investment. How can we consider anything a sacrifice when Christ has promised us that we will receive a reward that far supersedes the investment?

It seems as though human nature deduces that to give away that which we have means that we must ultimately do without those things that we desire to possess. But recall the conversation that Jesus and a few of His disciples were having one day.

> *Then Peter said to him, "We've given up everything to follow you. What will we get out of it?" 28And Jesus replied, "I assure you that when I, the Son of Man, sit upon my glorious throne in the Kingdom, you who have been my followers will also sit on twelve thrones, judging the twelve tribes of Israel. 29And everyone who has given up houses or brothers or sisters or father or mother or children or property, for my sake, will receive a hundred times as much in return and will have eternal life. (Matt 19:27–29 NLT)*

This conversation between the disciples—in particular Peter, who always seems to open mouth and insert
foot—was in response to a young barrister who seemed
curious about following Jesus, with whom he had no
doubt been impressed.

*¹⁶Then a man came to Jesus and said, "Teacher,
what good deed should I do to gain eternal
life?" ¹⁷Jesus said to him, "Why do you ask me
about what is good? There is only one who is
good. If you want to enter into life, obey the
commandments." ¹⁸"Which commandments?"
the man asked. Jesus said, "Never murder. Never
commit adultery. Never steal. Never give false
testimony. ¹⁹Honor your father and mother. Love
your neighbor as you love yourself." ²⁰The young
man replied, "I have obeyed all these commandments. What else do I need to do?" ²¹Jesus said
to him, "If you want to be perfect, sell what
you own. Give the money to the poor, and you
will have treasure in heaven. Then follow me!"
²²When the young man heard this, he went away*

sad because he owned a lot of property. (Matt 19:16–22 GWT)

In the valleys of life, we are often tempted to attend pity parties where we're the only ones in attendance. At such parties we tend to think about what we have given up; what we did not receive that, in our estimation, we deserve; and to resent those around us who have been blessed. One of the critical steps to navigating the valleys of life effectively is through our determination to give, to give generously, and to give by faith, expecting that God will honor His promises to all those who will obey Him. In so doing, we position ourselves to be recipients of God's interaction in our lives such that we not only survive the valleys but also emerge from them richer and wiser than when we entered that testing time in our lives.

Finally, let me say that the world is a messy place with many heartaches, pains, and tears; but heaven is but a heartbeat away. *Watch* for Him.

From the earliest days of my childhood, I have heard this old Southern Gospel song:

This world is not my home I'm just a passing through
My treasures are laid up somewhere beyond the blue
The angels beckon me from heaven's open door
And I can't feel at home in this world anymore
Oh Lord you know I have no friend like you
If heaven's not my home then Lord what will I do
The angels beckon me from heaven's open door
And I can't feel at home in this world anymore

Being a Southerner by birth and up-bringing, many such songs helped set the stage for my world-view long before I knew what a worldview was! For that upbringing, I will be eternally grateful for a focus that reaches beyond this temporal world and, by faith in God's Word sees the eternal, when we will rest from our labors in the presence of the One who directs all things good and holy.

But inherent to the heart of man is the understanding of an afterlife. Every civilization ever unearthed by archeologists has reflected that man *knew* there was a God. They might not have known the God *that is*, but they all knew that there *is* a God! Each civilization might have worshipped in sincerity, but any sincerity that is misplaced leads to eternal destruction rather than to life everlasting. This is the two-fold urgency with which each of us who are Christ followers must respond in obedience: our own time becomes increasingly brief with each passing day, and the eternity of a world without Christ looms closer.

From where you sit reading these words today to that place and time yet future when you will breathe your last breath, inescapable valleys await you. Neither you nor I can fully know what those valleys will entail. We might see them coming or awaken one morning to discover suddenly that we are surrounded by a valley. But to be sure, valleys do await us.

The importance of your encounter with the content of these pages might very well lie in the answer to the following question: Have you determined how you plan to face your valleys? Have you already chosen what attitudes you will reject as nonviable for you and which ones you plan to cultivate along your personal journey? I have both said and heard it said many times, "I cannot choose all the *circumstances* that come into my life, but I can choose the *attitude* with which I encounter my circumstances.

In one of the movies in the Indiana Jones series, both the good guys and the bad guys were racing in search of the Holy Grail. Both Indiana Jones and his nemesis had arrived before the keeper of the Grail and multiple choices confronted them. The old man's instruction was simple. Choose wisely.

You know, life is just that way, isn't it? We're faced with life-and-death decisions almost daily. We're also confronted with decisions about eternal life or eternal death. To choose wisely, according to the Bible, will lead to life everlasting. To discount the Scriptures without serious consideration (and acceptance) is perilous.

As Indiana Jones's nemesis grabbed and guzzled from one of the cups, rather than gaining what he had hoped for, he self-destructed as the adventuresome explorer and the keeper of the Grail looked on. Then came what must have been the most powerful line of the movie: "He didn't choose wisely!"

If there is a snowball's chance of a heaven and a hell, then it behooves every human being to consider seriously how one might proceed to gain the former and avoid the latter. If each of those two options is viable, as I believe they are, based upon the most enduring book of all human history—the Bible, God's Holy Word—then it *must* make a difference in the lives of those who read it. To dismiss it is unwise. To procrastinate in searching its pages is unwise. To fail to obey its instruction is unwise. To avoid its warning is unwise. To forget its promises is unwise. To forget its hope is unwise. We are compelled to consider, read, meditate on, memorize, and obey that precious old book that many people neglect, at which some might scoff, and which many will never hear— unless Christ followers are obedient to their commission.

Disobedient people go through valleys, but without the hope that trusting in Jesus Christ and obedience to His Word can bring. Tiger Woods, arguably the greatest golfer of all time, watched his world cave in upon him as the media exposed news of his multiple sexual affairs. In response to discussion in a Fox News broadcast during the early stages of that breaking tragic news, anchor Brit Hume nailed it when he declared that the best thing that Tiger Woods could do if he really wanted to turn it all around was to become a Christian, find the forgiveness that Jesus Christ offers, and discover how thereby he could make a successful comeback.

At the same time, obedient people will also go through valleys. To obey and follow Christ is not a "get out of jail free" card. Christ followers can expect to face the same dangers, tests, trials, and temptations that everyone else faces. The difference is that we can face them with a courage that is inherent to only those who truly trust God's Word. To the same degree that a believer in Christ fails to believe the promises of Christ, that individual becomes vulnerable to discouragement, and courage is soon replaced by fear.

For God hath not given us the spirit of fear; but of power, and of love, and of a sound mind. (2 Tim. 1:7)

During a conversation with one of my three sons (I've honestly forgotten whether it was Justin, Jordan, or Joshua) one day, I responded to a question he had asked with the thoughtless reply, "I'm doing well under the circumstances."

Instantly, he asked, "Why are you under the circumstances? You've always taught us that we're to be on top of our circumstances, Dad!"

I stood corrected. Taking our eyes off Jesus Christ, the author and finisher of our faith, will distract us and dilute our spiritual power every time, and we will soon find that we are "under the circumstances!"

The wise man Solomon once wrote,

"The spirit of a man shall sustain his infirmity; but a wounded spirit, who can bear? (Prov. 18:14)

It's at the very core of our thinking that we must choose, in advance, how we plan to progress when the trials, troubles, and tragedies of life come upon us. It becomes imperative that we choose to get knowledge, cultivate understanding, seek wisdom, and as the Boy Scouts of America are known for saying, "Be prepared."

In the console or glove box of most of our cars, SUVs, and trucks is a slip of paper known as a proof of insurance. We pay huge premiums for automobile insurance *just in case* we have an accident. We carry those papers along with our vehicle registrations *in the event of* an accident—or in the event that a member of law enforcement stops us and wants to chat! For many of us, we have never had to use the insurance, although a few of us have had occasion to offer our driver's license, registration, and proof of insurance to one of America's finest. We continue paying large sums of money annually *just in case* we might have an accident.

If we are wise to prepare in advance for events that might or might not ever come to pass, wouldn't it be the height of wisdom to prepare adequately for a guaranteed, inevitable event that each human being ever born of woman must face—death?

People die once, and after that they are judged. (Heb. 9:27 GWT)

I'm not sure that I have ever met a person who did not understand that people die. It's just a matter of time. Why would anyone who knows the inevitability of dying not seriously consider that reality and make wise preparation for what lies beyond, especially if there's the possibility of judgment. Although people might debate what kinds of judgment awaits (and I will forego a discussion dealing with the kind and timing of those judgments), isn't it foolish to fail to investigate and prepare?

Through the years, I have often said that a person is not really ready to live until he's prepared to die—and I believe that. The earlier in life that we make that preparation, the more time we will have to love and influence the lives of other people for God's glory. Also, it would seem that those who determine to follow Christ earlier rather than later in life would have fewer regrets by the end of life, assuming that theirs was a life well-lived, with a Christ like spirit and in service for Him.

Have you taken the first step of preparation for eternity by considering and accepting Jesus Christ as your personal Savior? If so, are you continuing that preparation each day as you allow him to be the Lord and director of your life? Or, as you seriously consider your future rendezvous with Him when you step from time into eternity, will you be ashamed, embarrassed to look into the eyes of the One who gave Himself for you?

You see, my friend, by the time it's all said and done, and the realities of either an eternity with God or an everlasting life without Him set in, the time for taking preparatory action will be past. Consider Him *today*!

As I type these words, I'm on a south-bound train from Soignies to Brussels, Belgium. I didn't sleep well last night because the travel details, including some loose ends, kept racing through my mind. I didn't want to oversleep for fear of missing my train. If I missed this train, then I would miss my plane to Chicago and ultimately not make the journey home tonight. Worry and sleeplessness notwithstanding, my host arrived to fetch me early. In spite of icy roads, we made it to the Soignies train station with several minutes to spare, and the long lines about which I had worried were not a problem. My host, Tim Downs, and I hugged goodbye.

A nighttime of worry did not help me make the train, but preparation and action did. I was almost completely packed for the journey before retiring for the night. An early awakening and less-than-casual grooming, dressing, and final packing, however, did help make the connection with time to spare.

When it's all said and done, life is something like taking a journey. We decide our destination. We purchase our ticket. We prepare. We get on-board. Finally, we arrive at the destination for which we made the plans.

In May 1959, when I understood that there are two possible destinations for a life after death, I decided that I had a choice between the two, and I'd much prefer heaven over hell. That Sunday morning, I accepted the ticket that had already been purchased on my behalf some two thousand years earlier. And one day—it could be any day—I will step aboard life's train for the final time. As it pulls into Heaven's Grand Central Station, I fully anticipate a gathering of family, friends, and total strangers to be on the platform when I step into the new world!

Years ago, I heard Dr. Vance Havner speak to a packed house—in those days about 4600 people for the Wednesday evening service—at the Thomas Road Baptist Church in Lynchburg, Virginia. He had given a thumbnail sketch of his life's story that night at the request of the late Dr. Jerry Falwell. Havner had told about his preference for train travel and how his father would take him as a young man to catch the trains as he journeyed to his preaching engagements, and how his "pap" would be there to meet him upon his return. The first thing Havner's father would ask him him was, "Well, son, how'd you make out?"

Similar to Dr. Havner, the accumulation of the years and the miles are growing for me, too. But one of these days, I'll step off the train—not in this world, but in the next. The journey of life will have ended, as will the opportunities to live for Christ in a world that needs salt and light that every child of God can offer. It is in this world that we make the investment of time, energy, resources, and influence. In the next, we find not only an eternal relationship in the very presence of God but also the reward for lives well-lived.

So, when it's all said and done, I want to have chosen well and lived well that I might please Him. Any reward gained will certainly be a bonus. And in those opening moments of eternity, somehow I believe that every heartache and valley of earth will evaporate from memory. Therefore, if one day these earthly trials, tests, and temptations will truly be worth it all, when we see Christ, why not use them now as a catalyst for serving—and for digging wells and leaving them in the valley?

Leave a well in the valley, the dark and lonesome valley;
Others have to cross this valley, too:
And what a blessing when they find the well of joy
you've left behind,
So, leave a well in the valley you go through.

Scriptures on Which to Meditate

(Hebrews 11:6 New International Version)

Without faith it is impossible to please God, because anyone who comes to him must believe that he exists and that he rewards those who earnestly seek him.

(Mark 11:24 Good News Translation)

When you pray and ask for something, believe that you have received it, and you will be given what you ask for.

(Romans 8:28 The New Testament in Modern English, J. B. Phillips)

Moreover we know that to those who love God, who called according to his plan, everything that happens fits into a pattern for good.

(2 Corinthians 1:8-11 The Living Bible)

We are crushed and over whelmed ... and saw how powerless we were to help ourselves; but that was good, for then we put everything into the hands of God ... for he can even raise the dead. And he did help ... and we expect him to do it again and again.

(1 Corinthians 2:9 The Living Bible)

No mere man has ever seen, heard, or imagined what wonderful things God has ready for those who love the Lord.

Epilogue

Although we cannot control the valleys that might come our way in life, we *can* control our attitudes and actions as we progress through whatever valleys the journey of life requires of us. The real-life stories that you have read in this book were shared for the sole purpose of letting you know that, although you might feel lonely as you navigate the temptations, tests, and trials of life, others have been there before you—and survived! You, too, can turn your buffetings into blessings as well, but you must *choose* to do so.

As you "dig" and "leave a well in the valley" through which you're going, I would love to hear your story of success. Write to me by visiting my website at www.dalepeterson.org.

If you are a pastor, in your pews each Sunday are hurting people. If I can help you minister God's grace to your congregation, contact me at www.dalepeterson.org.

LaVergne, TN USA
25 April 2010
180445LV00001B/2/P